Third Degree

Leadership,
Project Management &
Old-School Masonry

John R. Hill, Jr.

Third Degree

Leadership,
Project Management &
Old School Masonry

John R. Hill, Jr.

First Edition

ISBN 978-0-9911995-9-4

Hill Communication Services
www.HillCommSvc.com

Contents

Foreword / Introduction

This is a book about things I care about and about things practiced by many. It is a book about priorities, time management and values, cloaked in the habiliments of leadership, project management and Masonry.

Leadership is about developing a vision and setting a direction for a group, so that everyone can use some portion of the twenty-four hours in their day for the pursuit of a common goal.

Project Management is about monitoring, measuring and adjusting the collective energy of a group so that it can efficiently achieve a common outcome. This is to be done in a way that maximizes the use of the talents and resources available.

For me, Masonry is about

> doing the right thing,
> doing it for the right reason,
> doing it with the right people,
> and doing it to the best of your ability

For the masses, Masonry is a society of men focused on charitable work, maintaining moral uprightness and practicing brotherly love. Further, Masons engage in regular meetings containing rituals and secrets, which are exemplified in allegories and symbols.

In a Masonic lodge, at the opening and closing of a meeting and in the hour of a new member's initiation, it is duly noted that no Mason ever enters upon any great or important undertaking without first invoking the aid of Deity through prayer, for the purpose of focusing mind, energy and deed, on achieving improvement. This book is my prayer. So Mote It Be.

--*-*

James had progressed through the three degrees of Masonry, moving from darkness to light. First as an Entered Apprentice and then moving through the middle of the Masonic process as a Fellowcraft and relatively recently, he became a Master Mason. It was a year and a day ago, to be exact.

"Hello", said James.

"James, it's good to hear your voice. It's your Worshipful Master calling."

"Well hello Worshipful Master," James spoke a little hesitantly as he had not been a very active mason since joining the lodge. In total, James had attended two meetings, he was present at a Masonic Funeral and James and a guest attended the annual fundraising dinner dance. This was the extent of his participation in lodge activities.

"How are you and how's the j-o-b?" said the Worshipful Master.

"Fine, Worshipful Master, everything's just fine."

"James, I'll get right to the point. I'd like for you to take on a small but special project for me."

"Yes," James said, only acknowledging the conversation and not meaning he would do the work.

The Worshipful Master continued, "As you probably know we have recently started an Entered Apprentice class for men who have been approved to join the lodge and I'm happy to say Samuel Gordon, an up and coming member of our community and a senior vice president in his company, is joining our ranks the good old-fashioned way! I think his corporate position and name recognition presents a unique opportunity to capture the story behind his entry into Masonry. I am hoping the story will provide some insight to our community regarding how to achieve life balance when engaged in a major leadership role and actively participating in Masonry. Brother James, I'm thinking that we can put your degree in English to good use and that you are the best person in our lodge to handle the task of documenting how a member of the Masonic craft can balance their professional leadership role and Masonry."

"My hope is that we can do one or maybe both of two things with the story you author," he added. "First, you can write the article for our own local magazine for all of the Masons in our three-county region to read. You do get and read our magazine don't you?"

"Yes, I do Worshipful Master."

"Second, I'd also like for us to consider passing on the article to our state Grand Lodge so they can publish the same article or the same basic information in the statewide journal. It's been a long time since our lodge has contributed anything to the state journal and I'd like to reinforce our commitment toward the efforts of Grand Lodge by actively providing more support. James, can you help me and the lodge out?"

"Yes sir, I do believe I can." said James.

"James, I do have a third outcome for this endeavor," commented the Worshipful Master. "I need you to listen to and take to heart the leadership messages that Brother Gordon will share with you. I have met many men who are in leadership positions, that don't quite measure up to the task, but Brother Samuel Gordon is the real deal. I believe with your natural talents and the sharing of information with Brother Gordon, you can strengthen your knowledge and position yourself for a leadership role in the Lodge. Do you have any questions?" But after a short pause, not quite long enough for James to ask a question. The Worshipful Master continued, "I will arrange for you and Brother Gordon to meet, probably in a couple of weeks, as I know Brother Gordon has some work-related travel on the horizon. You can develop the article in any style that is comfortable for you. I only ask that the end product is informative on the balance between masonry and leadership or something close to that general theme. If you have any questions, you have my contact information, feel free to use it." After another small pause, even shorter than the first, he added, "another option is to come by and visit me at a lodge meeting."

James could feel the warm smile on the Worshipful Master's face, over the phone. The Worshipful Master's smile was present for many reasons, but primarily because he knew that James was a good man, and would be a better man and Mason if he was engaged in the activities of the fraternity.

"James, I didn't really give you time to ask anything. Do you have any questions?"

"No sir, nothing at this time."

--*-*

After a couple of weeks, the Worshipful Master arranged for their first meeting. Prior to the meeting James learned that Samuel had received his Masonic first degree seven weeks earlier and that he had attended four of five study classes. Samuel had also met with the dean of the class once and worked with his classmates at their homes twice. So it seemed to James that Samuel was dedicated to the learning process. He could tell that Samuel was putting in the time and making an effort to learn the work of the craft and to develop an understanding of the values that make masonry, masonry.

*_*_*_*

If you have a desire to lead or you are already a leader, you will see tools and ideas on these pages to help you refine your skills and become a better leader. You will find value in the dialogue between Samuel and James as they discuss leadership concepts. There is something to be gained from the Deeper into Leadership sections which share thoughts and ideas regarding leading within and outside of Masonry. Learning the tools of Project Management will help you to organize the work and efforts of a team so that they can perform at their best. Using any or all of the messages in this book is an act of self improvement and self improvement will make you a better leader.

Your leadership skills can support your day-to-day life both inside and outside of the work environment. You will find ideas and tips to help better coordinate getting things done with your family, friends and acquaintances, in church, at work and other places. In your personal engagements and other endeavors, you will increase your rate of success when you utilize the tools of project management. With project management tools you will be more efficient and the people around you will work in a more coordinated fashion.

There is something mystical and beautiful about the men of Masonry and the way we conduct ourselves to advance the manner in which we honored our God, our family, our neighbors and ourselves. Following the Masonic example of continuous self improvement and supporting the needs of others is a model of successful leadership. This model of leadership is not a secret of Masonry and is worth sharing. You will become a better man or woman for reading this book and utilizing its teachings. The goal is to make use of the Masonic framework and the information on leadership and project management to continuously explore creating positive changes in you and in others. Like all good leaders and Masons, we will fervently engage to always and vigilantly strive to be a better, more perfect person.

Mason's often say we take good men and make them better. This book is written so you can move from your present place to a better place.

Chapter One ~ Entered Apprentice

James remembers from his youth, the mystique of Masonry and how he consistently met good, positive and active men who were Masons. He remembers seeing the men with big black cases, hanging around the house. They were engaged in positive activities around the neighborhood.

Some of these men and masons were bankers, officers of the law and courts, laborers, doctors, and business owners. Regardless of their backgrounds, they carried themselves with dignity, which let you know they were about something. Even if you did not know exactly what they were doing, because they did not often talk publically about their good works, you knew and saw that when important things were happening in the community the masons were around. James knew if there was an injustice and his parents or grandparents called on the masons, the injustice would be confronted. These men gathered behind closed doors, as an outsider he may not have known what was taking place behind those doors, but whatever it was, it was important and it made positive things happen.

A big part of what happens behind those closed doors is teaching, training and sharing information about success, leadership, and management. We focus this learning in tangible ways by dispensing charity, showing honor for God and tending to the needs of our immediate families, neighbors and others in the Masonic family.

Chapter 1 - Entered Apprentice

--*-*

"So, Brother Gordon, I am going to open up with the same basic question each time we meet, which is: What have you learned recently in Masonry that aligns with your professional and leadership responsibilities?"

Samuel thought for a moment, and then replied. "I have five things that come to mind." He rattled off each, while flicking his fingers until his hand was wide open.

1.) Be on time.
2.) Work hard.
3.) Be prepared.
4.) Know the goal.
5.) Love what you do.

"You don't mind if I take notes do you?" asked James.

Samuel replied with a big grin on his face, "I'd be concerned if you didn't take notes."

After scratching a few notes, James said, "So why start with 'Be on time?'"

"Generally, it is my perception that you need to be present to have an impact. A former boss told me, 'If you have to choose, it is better to be 15 minutes early, than 1 minute late.' I have never forgotten that lesson. Samuel continues, from my lodge initiation, I remember hearing about equal regularity; I haven't gotten deep into that subject in my studies, but I remember enough to have internalized this statement to be about Masons being on time. I have seen that our Worshipful Master has a policy of starting on time, no matter what. He attended one of our study sessions and the dean of our study class was waiting for one or two people. At the hour we were planning to start, I could hear the Worshipful Master whisper in the dean's ear that he needed to start the study class on time. So the dean quickly called us to prayer and we began our study class. That concern for the time of the people present was directly in line with my corporate practice of starting meetings on time."

"I also remember a manager I admire, who intentionally began her meetings with the most important news that she had to share. She would not repeat the information twice, so people quickly learned to be on time."

After a brief pause, James asked, "What about your second item, Work hard?"

Samuel replied, "Almost nothing replaces hard work and persistence while striving for success. There are lots of clichés and quotes that fit, like it takes extreme pressure over many years to create a diamond or Barbara Jordan's words – 'There is no obstacle in the path of young people who are poor, or members of minority groups, that hard work and preparation cannot cure.' Samuel continued, Vince Lombardi said 'The dictionary is the only place that success comes before work. Hard work is the price we must pay for success. I think you can accomplish anything if you're willing to pay the price.' All of these examples reinforce the idea that hard work is how you create the path to success."

"Thanks," James said, "I find the third item on the list, 'Be prepared' to be interesting.

Samuel responded, "Well actually, in hindsight, I would put 'Know the goal' before 'Be prepared'. Mostly because I think it's important to know what you are preparing for. I believe having goals is critical to success. Many years ago, I read the Harvard success study, where they measured the success of the Business School's class of 1979. They asked who in the class had goals, and then asked who had written goals and a plan to accomplish those goals. Ten years later, the class members that had goals were making twice as much as the group that had no goals. The class members that had written goals and a plan were making 10 times as much! I'm not saying that money is the best measure of success, but it reinforced for me that having a goal is better than not having a goal, and having a goal that is written and a plan to achieve that goal, is an additional plus."

James listened and took notes as Samuel continued, "Being prepared is where opportunity turns into success. In the Lodge, one of my motivations is to not be embarrassed when reciting the work we need to memorize. I know the way for me not to be embarrassed is to put in the time and to be prepared. Memorizing information isn't necessarily what I signed up for, but after Brother Young shared with me that the reason we study and commit the information to memory is so that we internalize the values of the organization. That made sense to me, and because of my desire to be a good man and Mason like my grandfather, I'm in this all the way."

"Tell me about your grandfather." asked James.

"In my eyes, he was great. I enjoyed his spirit, his intensity for life, his ability to take charge when necessary. He was able to serve the needs of the people around him, and in his own way he had the ability to expound wisdom at just the right time and place. All this from a man who was generally reserved, maybe even a little shy."

"My granddad was at one point the Worshipful Master of his lodge," Samuel said thoughtfully. "I asked him about being Worshipful Master. He shared, 'There is a natural evolution to leadership in a well-governed and supported Masonic Lodge. There is a progression of positions.' In most lodges you progress from a Stewart, to a Master of Ceremony, to a Deacon, to a Warden and then to Worshipful Master. My Grandfather said he held all of those offices. When you progress through the offices, you learn more about the organization, the duties and responsibilities of the many roles in the organization and how they all interrelate."

Samuel kept going, immersed in the memory of the lessons his grandfather had passed on to him.

"My Grandfather then told a story about watching my growth at a local store and how it relates to a natural progression of roles," he said, 'you were a decent student, polite, and at the age where you should begin working. Your dad asked if I knew someone who would give you a job and I knew a local department store owner, who I gave a call. As a result, with no interview, you were told to report for work on Saturday morning!"

"On your arrival you were greeted warmly shown the offices, stock rooms, bathroom, lunchroom and other parts of the facility. You were then handed a broom and told to sweep the floor in the main showroom and stockroom. You swept and mopped, and scrubbed and polished and cleaned, from what I recall based on your complaints, you thought you cleaned every inch of the property. You raked, you washed sidewalks, you fixed windows, installed shelves and performed other tasks that were new to you. But the team at the store offered guidance and help, and graciously accepted the broken glass, the spilled can of paint, and the torn curtains. This maintenance role went on for three or four months and then gradually they started having you perform inventory tasks, restocking shelves, and moving seasonal items. Slowly, without any prompting, you began to become more engaged on the floor, answering customer questions. 'Young man, where can I find cleaning products?' 'Do you have this in another color?' 'Is this the correct size for a swimming pool?' Soon enough, you were a regular on the floor, and some other new guy was cleaning every nook and cranny of the shop. Didn't miss that work did you? But every now and then, when the store wasn't busy or something needed to be done, you would do it, just because it was the right thing to do. With more experience, you gained the skills and knowledge to work the register, open and close the store, and handle other management tasks, Then, all too soon, it was off to college."

After sharing his Grandfathers story, Samuel said, "The lesson was that to evolve into a good team member, I needed to understand the place. So I learned where everything was while cleaning, I learned how to move merchandise to the front and what was in inventory on the back shelves. I learned how the inventory moved from season to season. This knowledge made me a good team member when working on the floor of the store. From this I have observed that many good managers have developed a good understanding of the operation from the ground floor, up."

"An evolution of knowledge is what enables the maturation of a Mason or leader. When bringing an individual into the organization. Give them the ground floor background and information they need to understand the organization. Followed by a series of assignments that will provide the opportunity and information they need to experience the operations of the organization. This will enable an individual to exercise that knowledge when they are in a leadership role. The outcome will be someone who can advance the good works of the organization, maintain the harmony of the same and enable others to make a similar advance."

"Thank you, that was a wonderful story, I hope to be able to use it somehow in the article," James then asked. "Finally, from your list, 'Love what you do.'"

"Well, this one is the bedrock of the list," Samuel said. "Being a leader takes you in all kinds of unexpected directions and will cause you to re-prioritize your life. It will mess with your schedule and you will deal with things that you believe to be trivial, unimportant, unnecessary or just plain stupid. You had better love what you do, so you can consistently give the role the energy it needs. So you can be creative, so you can read that extra e-mail, write that extra note or make that extra call. Loving the work makes it easier and makes it a more enjoyable activity, rather than another dreary task yet to be completed. If you love what you do, you will perform it in an authentic way. In a way that is genuinely you and that authenticity will come through to all the people you connect with while in the role of leader."

James spoke, "Well, thanks for that break down, I'm sure it will be helpful. Remember, I'll ask the same starting question next time we meet. Moving slightly in another direction, how do you balance work and home with Masonry?"

"Well, until recently, the balancing act didn't include Masonry, but primarily it goes back to having goals," said Samuel. "I personally know what is important to me and I do the things necessary to be successful at those things. When it comes to home, not much takes priority. I do what I can to plan out all the home activities so I know what I have to do and when. I assure that I invest in the maintenance of relationships that define my home life. As much as possible, I try to prevent emergencies. But no matter how much anyone tries, there are emergencies and my response is the same when it comes to home. I stop whatever I am doing and attend to home. No ifs, ands, or buts. I use technology to limit the time necessary to get control of the situation, but when technology doesn't work, I leave were I am and I go to where the emergency exists. Balance for me is only possible when home is ok."

Samuel continues, "So far my learning in Masonry is that my family and profession come first and that aligns with my personal priorities and makes me comfortable being part of the organizations. When the Brothers came to my home for my investigation, they insisted that my partner be present. The reason, as you know, was so they could share with her that being a Mason would take time. They failed to mention the money and energy, but I forgive the oversight." They both smile. "Anyway, even though the expectation was that I would give time to Masonry, it was also that I should not prioritize Masonry over my family and that I should never lose sight of my responsibilities to home, worship and work. But even with that being the case, it would mean time away from the family. They asked if my family felt that they could support my efforts to be a better man and if they felt comfortable sharing time with the Lodge. That conversation reinforced for me that my Masonic activities would impact my schedule, but it also set the expectation for me and my family that they could still depend on me at home.

At the same investigation meeting, they shared that Masonry is a journey, not to be rushed, but to be invested in consistently and over a long period of time, so Masonry does not required that a man lose sight of his family priority, but only that he is willing to commit parts of his discretionary time to Masonry and that he is flexible in his use of discretionary time to help his Brothers and their activities.

When joining Masonry you should have control of a good amount of discretionary time, for the process demands time, but from the time of your full introduction into the Lodge, your efforts in support of your lodge will ebb and flow. Your major task will be to mean yes when you say yes, and to be comfortable saying no when time does not permit. Balancing your nos and yeses is as important, as balancing your use of time.

Deeper into Leadership

In each chapter, the "Deeper into Leadership" section will highlight practical leadership philosophy including a Worshipful Master's leadership role and perspective. Here, we'll start with several strategy development based concepts and continue this section by talking about activities associated with starting a project and building the right kind of team.

When a Worshipful Master establishes his trestle board or more commonly stated, his leadership plan, he must advance two concepts: The first concept is creating a vision, and the second concept is enabling the culture to execute the vision. The Worshipful Master may not solely create and enable the creation of the vision and execution of the vision in the organization. However, for the organization to be effective, both the vision and execution must be achieved. If the Worshipful Master only creates the vision and is not the enabler of the execution to achieve the vision, then he is a thought leader. If the Worshipful Master enables the execution of the vision from a previous administration or it is authored by others, like the Grand Lodge, then he is an operational leader. If the Worshipful Master's efforts and energy support the creation of the vision and enables the execution of the tasks necessary to achieve the vision, he is the guiding force for the organization. Guiding force leadership is the dimension of leadership that we will continue to explore.

Strategic Planning

A definition I use for a strategic plan is it is a documented, coordinated and disciplined set of activities and processes created to help a team produce a desired outcome in the future.

As a leader you have the responsibility to communicate direction and priorities to those whom you will lead. This communication should encompass the different levels of information needed by the people on the team. The objective is to create a set of documents that will enable all members of the organization to visualize its goals. As leader you may or may not be expected to author this full set of documents. In either case you have a vested interest in the content and quality of all the documents and therefore if you do not author all parts of the documentation, you do want to see and comprehend the information in all documents that are created to express the organizations vision.

A strategic plan has a long time horizon and is achieved as a result of many projects and other organizational activities. A strategic plan is not achieved with a single project. Usually the time frame of the strategic plan is more than a year. Typically the view is 3 to 5 years and ambitious organizations and leaders use longer horizons like 10, 25 or 50 years. An old school African tradition is to consider your actions and plans relative to their impact in seven generations. That's 140 years!

The word "documented" is a critical component of the definition because if your thoughts and ideas are not documented, they are less helpful for a team and more applicable to personal use. Your undocumented thoughts do not represent a tool to be used by a team to identify a coordinated and disciplined process. Those undocumented thoughts cannot easily help a team to produce a desired outcome. So be sure to document your strategic plan to make it a more valuable tool for long range planning and activity.

Another aspect of a strategic plan is that its scope normally encompasses the entire organization. All of the team members should feel connected to the strategy and therefore its universality demands that the plan is relevant throughout the enterprise.

Representing a broad view of an organization requires engaging a cross section of its members. Many Worshipful Masters announce their independently created trestle boards with poor results, rather than working with their officers and members to develop the strategic plan. This independent thought can lead to a lack of team member commitment and a lack of engagement and support for the implementation of the strategic plan.

A final thought before looking at the details of a strategic plan is that you should not create a strategic plan for the mere fact of having a strategic plan. Its value is achieved when it is a living document upon which organizational decisions are to be based. Therefore, the organization must be vigilant in referencing the strategic plan and it should enable the team to internalize it content. The organization should consistently reference it's projects and other activities back to the strategic plan to verify alignment. The organization should measure progress based on the goals articulated in the strategic plan. Adjust the projects, activities or strategic plan to improve the organizations alignment.

A Strategic Plan Outline

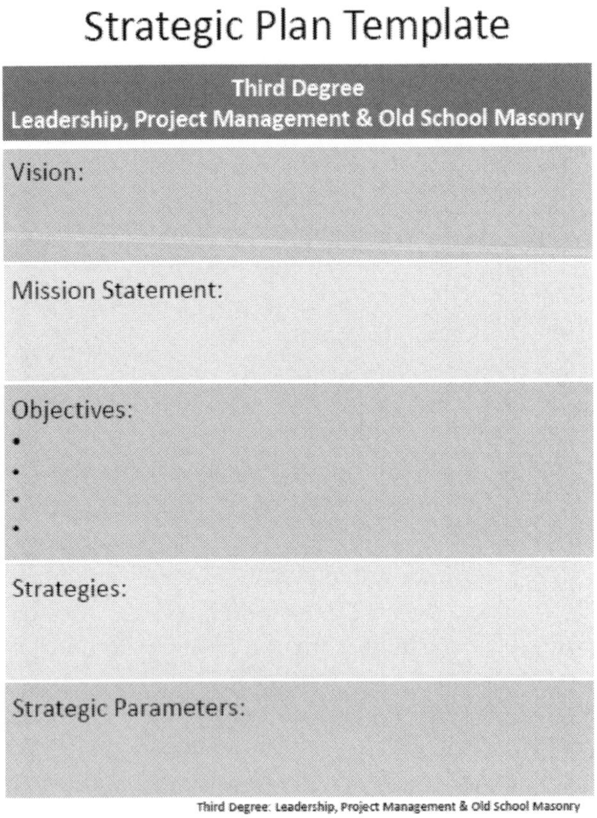

Strategic Plan Template

Third Degree Leadership, Project Management & Old School Masonry
Vision:
Mission Statement:
Objectives: • • • •
Strategies:
Strategic Parameters:

Third Degree: Leadership, Project Management & Old School Masonry

Figure 1: Strategic Plan Template

The objective of setting the strategy as documented in a strategic plan is to set the values and moral compass for the organization. After reading the strategic plan, members of the team should be able to shape their actions to be in alignment with the guiding principles of the organization. An effective strategy will answer, what is important to the organization, who the organization serves, what the organization delivers and how it does it. The strategic plan will set the vision for what the future looks like.

Strategic Planning is more art than science. As an art it is beautiful to behold when done well. At its most beautiful the plan transcends any changes in leadership and supports the fundamentals of the organization. It is developed via an assessment of where you are and how you arrived, followed by stating your direction and plans for action.

Beliefs/Vision

> A belief/vision statement is a formal expression of the organization's fundamental values; its ethical code, its overriding convictions, its inviolate commitments.

> The belief/vision should not change frequently after it is established. It should pass from one generation to the next generation with only small and necessary adjustments made along the way. For Masons, our belief system is captured in our ritual and our practices. For many organizations, their values can be found in the reason they were created and who they serve.

Mission Statement

> A mission statement is a statement that is written in a clear and concise fashion, to express the outcomes that are important to an organization. In addition a well written mission statement will articulate the organizations competitive advantages. Your competitive

advantage leads to what this organization will do better than anyone else, in the same arena, to help its customers and to be successful.

Objectives

The objectives are the organization's commitment to achieve specific and measurable results. Identify what market you are serving. Describe the customer needs you will address. Say how the world will be better because you exist.

Strategies

Strategies are the most important part of the planning process. They are the stated actions and resources the organization will utilize to meet its mission and objectives.

Strategic Parameters

Strategic parameters state the self imposed cultural direction for the organization. These are the things the organization will never do or will always do. The intent of these parameters is to give direction to the team members of the things that to organization values and should not be sacrificed on the road to achieving the mission and objectives.

The strategic plan creation process starts with an assessment of the current state of the organization and when there is a rich history for the organization the assessment includes a reflection on the things the organization has inherited from its past. This current state analysis is reflected in the Vision/Beliefs. Following the current state analysis is the documentation of the future the organization envisions for itself, which are articulated by the mission, strategy and objectives. Organizational truths are documented within the Strategic Parameters to reflect the cultural construct within which the organization will work. You then share the message with every member of the organization and complete the process by constant and consistent evaluation of how you are executing against your strategy.

Your execution against the strategy is frequently achieved by resourcing a series of projects that will when completed support the achievement of the measurable components of your objectives. Each project, which has a beginning and an end, will have a Project Charter which identifies that role of the project and its specific achievements. The collective set of projects is designed to achieve the vision, but at the implementation level teams most focus on executing the work immediately in front of them with excellence. Therefore the project charter gives guidance on the specific deliverables and content for the immediate work to be performed. Project charters will be detailed in the Project Management Tools of this chapter.

The next level in the documentation set is a roadmap, which outlines the sequence of projects and events that the organization plans to execute in support of the vision and mission. It is most often represented as a graphic image; however a prose description or a list of projects is acceptable. At its best the roadmap shows sequence and interrelationships between activities. The important goal regarding the roadmap is that it provides the context for how all efforts and events are connected.

After the roadmap is established, the next level down is to communicate the details of each project in a project charter. Normally an individual activity on the roadmap is a project. Another attribute of a project and its representation on the roadmap, is it always has a beginning and an end. This attribute is important, because it structures the sequence of activities and promotes one observable measurement of the progress of the organization. A project charter, the written overview of the project is the lowest level document we will define in the hierarchy of documents a leader should manage to align the efforts of the team.

Hiring Good People

Find good people with the right skills. Equally important is to find people who love the work that your organization performs and has the personality to mesh well with your organization. Then endeavor to create a balanced team by putting together these skilled individuals in a way that will make their collective thought robust, which can make success easier to achieve. Balance is achieved with a diversity of backgrounds, thoughts and experiences to name a few measures. It's easy to want to select people just like yourself and your circle of friends, but, not on the team should be like you. Find people who think in different and broader or narrower perspectives. Choose people who will not always say yes. Note, I did not say find someone who will always challenge you. The selection is not about finding someone who is fundamentally your opposite. In rare occasions that can be beneficial to shake things up. But you want to find people who are smart, have a positive way of thinking and who are not afraid to express their opinions. Their thought processes and concerns regarding some of the assumptions that have for historic reasons become a part of the culture. Some things that were good for yesterday and even today, may not be as valuable and may even be unhealthy in the future. Find people who can spot those changes and can provide ideas on how to move forward.

So, how do you hire good people?

1.) Know what you need, exactly.

It's easier said than done, but this cannot be over stated. Determining the skills and other attributes necessary to satisfactorily perform the job should not be relegated to the HR department. Each person you bring to the team will make plenty of decisions that will improve the group or negatively impact the group.

You need to understand the important skills, related to the assignment and team membership. Use your network of previous job holders and customers that have interacted with the role and the team. Talk to peers. From this set of dialogues and your own perceptions, document the details of your needs from the person who will fill this assignment, so that you can spot them a mile away and easily determine when they are not present in the person you will interview. Your goal is to only hire the best people.

The defined set of skills and capabilities should be broad enough to be enduring, it should also be perfect for now and directionally correct in its path to the future. You and the people you hire must be adaptable to change.

In addition to the important skills, you should have a deep understanding and plan for what activities this individual will perform what they must learn and the position in the organization they must fill.

2.) Recruit

Transfer your expectations of the assignment to a job description, electronic posting and your network of friends and business associates. I like to answer the 'How will their performance be measured?' question early, so people can self-exclude themselves from the process if they know they can't measure up to the expectations.

There is one additional comment in the recruiting space. Many of the top candidates enter the job search process very inquisitively, but not necessarily looking for a specific job title or to be with a specific company. They enter looking for a way to broaden and/or advance their career. So be willing to just talk to people and network, and offer opportunities on an exploratory basis. If you provide good information there is a possibility you can find just the right person without anyone having to create or find a matching job title.

3.) Identify good candidates

You know what you are looking for and many people have presented themselves as possessing what you need. Identifying the appropriate individual is the process of extracting from them proof that they have what you seek. This should not be taken lightly, and you should not feel restricted (other than by the laws of the land) in your search for the truth.

Testing is acceptable. If you need a person to handle accounting, give them an accounting problem to solve. If you need a salesperson, make them sell. If you need clerical work and proficiency with a word processor, have them type. If you need presentation skills, make them give a presentation. Know exactly what you want and verify they can produce what you want.

4.) Check references and involve the team

More eyes on the subject are better than a single pair. Reaching out to people who have had previous contact with the person in question can be an invaluable way of getting a better picture of the person. In addition, asking your colleagues, peers, and associates, to participate in the selection process can expose information that you may be blind to for any number of reasons. Exposing the individual to people he or she will work with or customers they will serve can be a valuable reference point.

Once you have built a strong team, you must let them perform with a certain amount of independence and you must provide them opportunities to input on the growth of the team.

Depending on your style and time availability, you can allow your team to pre-screen or post-screen candidates. Always holding the final decision yourself but allowing constructive input from your current team members.

Hire good people and recognize them for being good.

It is said and I believe that creating a great team is the sign of a great leader.

Servant hood

Since you have focused on the mechanics of setting a vision and discussed creating a strategic plan, project charter and hiring a quality team, let's turn inward with introspection and talk about a leader's personal motivation.

The path to becoming an empathetic leader is for you to have known how to be a good follower. You will have to have empathy for those who are in a following role.

The thing that many Worshipful Masters have learned regarding leadership during his progression through lodge positions is that often leading is best accomplished with an attitude of servant hood. Beginning from a brother's first leadership role, the objective is service to his lodge. In likewise fashion you should first seek to serve and as you meet the needs of your constituency, you will evolve to your natural position of leadership.

Servant based leadership is helping people to meet their needs, while serving the greater good of the organization. It's about taking a group of people to a common place where everyone can contribute their time, talents, and resources to help the group achieve its desired objective.

Successful Worshipful Masters help the lodge to execute in a consistent and common way on a road that is commonly understood by all who support the goals of the lodge. Each member will contribute what they can, sometimes investing a lot and sometimes not. Your service to the team is to enable an experience where independent of the size of the investment there will be a common experience that brings the members closer together. Because everyone has a deep understanding of the goals of the lodge the team will have synergy and their closeness will enable them to more easily grow toward the larger goals of the lodge.

The servants' role of a Worshipful Master is to consolidate the efforts and skills of the entire team to achieve something positive. Having learned the responsibilities and the skills necessary to achieve success through the many roles that have been held personally and through providing assistance during servant leadership experiences, the leader is capable of making positive decisions regarding using all the talents of the team. When the team is cohesive and the mission is enduring and focused, there is a coherence and power that will emanate from the lodge. When the mission is just a collective good can be fully achieved.

One objective for a successful leader is to elevate their meetings from that of being a crowd of voices and discussions, to an active set of hands engaged in creating and building. This action, activity and effort based on the goals of the organization are the best way to deliver results. Many lodges, companies, organizations, and volunteer groups, never get past the banter in their meetings and sometimes even worse the gossip and rumors mill that surround their meetings. Your responsibility as a servant to the team is to take the good and powerful discussions, beyond the dialogue stage and into the execution of the great ideas that support the organizations goals.

Another expanse of your job as a servant leader is to define the boundaries of the work efforts and to assist in the management of the processes that enable the work to be completed. You serve by being a cheerleader and helping the team members to have their needs met by supporting their successes and failures. Failures are a way for the team to stretch and grow. The growth comes from solving the organizational problems generated by the failure. Serve by finding ways to be present and support the good work and effort of the team, while also providing the necessary reprimands and corrections when organizational directives, policies and rules are not followed. Be ready to provide coaching when others do not know or follow the organizational norms, are not meeting expectations and are falling short of the team's objectives.

Being a good servant leader is all about being prepared to serve by enabling the team and yourself to get what they need, while producing the results that support the organization's goals.

Mentors

Be a mentor as a way to express your servant leadership responsibility. Mentorship is sharing information, your perspective and experiences, so that another individual can build upon and incorporate your insights into their personal style.

Mentoring is a very specific servant leadership activity that enables you to invest in another person. This investment is different than focusing on a project or the goals of an organization. The investment is a purely servant hood engagement.

The mentoring relationship works best when the connection is with a person whom you have a positive rapport. So as a mentor, be positive, be open, be someone who a subordinate can be comfortable with and can confidently confide. Be someone who is open to understand people's uniqueness and talk to them about how they can integrate and excel at the organization. Provide information that be used to help them grow positive relationships.

How to be a mentor! Be available for conversations on a regular basis. The agenda can be structured and formal or the conversation can be freewheeling. Just sharing the time and information is the highest order function in a mentor/mentee relationship.

As a mentor, to excel beyond the basic everyday run-of-the-mill mentor relationship, find ways and opportunities to help people succeed in meeting their dreams and career aspirations. The best mentee will be a person you trust and respect, and you can therefore make recommendations for them to perform growth assignments, engage in learning opportunities and you can providing networking experiences that will enable your mentee to grow. These types of support actions are a positive way to let the relationship grow beyond the norm.

If you are the mentee, make things easy on your mentor. Be prepared based on the agreement you both have made. Be early to sessions. Be ready to initiate conversations, with comments, questions and stories about you, your work, your dreams and goals. Be ready to get the conversation started. Manage time so that your session ends at the agreed time.

As a leader, consider making an investment in developing your mentoring skills by mentoring a person and assisting them to explore their abilities and skills. This type of relationship is rewarding for both parties.

Project Management Tools

Project Management tools are used to coordinate the efforts of an organization. The tools discussed in this section will be Project Charter, WISDOM, the 5 W's, and SWOT. With good and reasonable insight a team can utilize these four tools to better understand the execution of the early parts of team execution.

Project Charter

One of the early documents created is the mission statement. The mission statement expresses the highest level of direction for the organization. A mission statement is a written expression of the desired future state of an organization. The desired outcome is orchestrated to be achieved after the successful completion of all envisioned projects and any additional ongoing team efforts. It is a vivid description of what the future will be like and should inspire the beneficiaries to invest in its execution and to provide their talent, knowledge, skills and efforts. The mission statement is to be made visible and well known to everyone in the organization. It should be include as part of the initial training when joining the organization and reiterated frequently. Senior leadership should speak often of the mission statement at various gatherings and include key components of the mission statement in regular communication. The objective is to make the mission statement a regular part of the vocabulary of the team.

Project Charter

A project charter is a narrative description of the project objectives.

Project Charter Outline

- Paragraph 1: Project Justification
    - Business Need, Business Opportunity
- Paragraph 2: Results expected
    - Target Market
- Paragraph 3: Deliverables
    - Schedule
- Paragraph 4: Success Measures
- Paragraph 5: Constraints
- Paragraph 6: Team Members (Roles)

Third Degree: Leadership, Project Management & Old School Masonry

Figure 2: Project Charter Outline

When properly written and concurred, the project charter provides directional guidance. It structures the expectations for the team and provides guidance in a way similar to the North Star or a lighthouse. The guidance enables everyone to consistently make independent decisions and perform their roles without taking the project off course.

Requirements for a project charter are that they are written, published and made visible in ways to make them available for frequent reference: posters, flyers, opening statements at the beginning of every meeting, backgrounds for computer screens, banners for web sites, etc.

A unifying way to start a project is for a team to develop their project charter. This means hosting sessions to discuss the content and develop a broad set of options before selecting the final content. In a mature organization, the charter is not a static document, and is maintained and modified as necessary. When changes are required they should be communicated far and wide. Changes to the charter should be treated as a major event in the life of the project and should only occur to enhance the ultimate direction and success of the project. Trivial details are to be managed elsewhere.

It is a document that provides the project participants with a description of the project and the outcomes that will make the organization better.

A project charter is an early step in organizing the responsibilities and execution actions of a larger operation. It includes the alignment of your vision, identifies the reason for the project, the project's organization, plan for implementation and your list of known risks and success measures.

The vision component of the project charter can state the scope of the project, i.e., what the project will accomplish and what is its focus. It should give some understanding as to why the project exists and call out the guiding principles for the project, including assumptions that exist as fundamental to the execution of the project. A good vision provides guidance both about what a project is, and what it is not. The reasons for the project should directly relate to the scope of the project and identify the business case for the project.

The implementation plan should identify the people, process and technology that will be employed in the implementation of the project. Stating milestones, dates when specific tasks will be completed, will enable monitoring the progress of the activity and support making corrections or decisions on the continued investment in the project.

Round out the document by investing in a discussion of risks and success measures. Acknowledging risks can enable the team to mitigate the risks and prevent them for occurring or the team can better respond when a risk turns into a problem.

Knowing the success measures early in the project, will enable the team to properly adjust as they progress through the life cycle of the project.

With these documents in place and when properly shared, the leader will have accomplished the task of setting direction and priorities for the organization.

W-I-S-D-O-M

In Masonry, it's said that the Worshipful Master, through his progression in lodge leadership and organizational roles, has developed the wisdom to lead; he thus has the responsibility for sharing this wisdom as he supports lodge activities and all of the lodge's engagements. The Worshipful Master has gained his status of leader because the process has opened WISDOM to him, and as he became fully engaged in the activities of the lodge he acquired the teaching of W-I-S-D-O-M:

W = Work

> "Leaders aren't born they are made. And they are made just like anything else, through hard work. And that's the price we'll have to pay to achieve that goal, or any goal."
>
> Vince Lombardi

The success of programs and charitable endeavors of a lodge are not achieved by chance or happenstance; it is the deliberate effort of the many involved. As a leader, chairmen, president, it will be your job to orchestrate the themes and set the direction for the group. You are to allocate the work effort, as success is achieved through the proper execution of hard work. As the work progresses you are to praise the successes and you must in the most tender manner correct the failures. You are to choreograph the hard work that will lead to the achievement of the goal.

I = Integrity

> "Real integrity is doing the right thing, knowing that nobody's going to know whether you did it or not."
>
> Oprah Winfrey

Lead with integrity and lead with the high moral character becoming the venerable institution of Masonry.

It is not acceptable to forsake the ethics and values of Masonry or your organization, for the expedience of satisfying today's needs or for any other reason. As leaders we are as good as our reputations and the values upon which our reputations are built.

S = Study

> "In seed time learn, in harvest teach, in winter enjoy."
>
> William Blake

As a leader you should improve your education consistently, ever improving yourself and striving for perfection. Be always ready to assist others to learn the skills of your profession.

D= Dialogue

> "A lecture is much more of a dialogue than many of you probably realize."
>
> Samuel Wald

As a leader you must seek out the wise counsel of others, ask questions and consider what is said. Constructive dialogue allows you to make quality decisions. Give credit to those involved in the success of those decisions, and be ready to protect them when trouble arises. Growth through the exchange of knowledge and information is the path forward. Additionally be ready to pay it forward, be ready to whisper wise counsel to those in need and who are ready and in the proper position to receive that counsel.

O = Optimize

> To achieve great things, two things are needed:
> A plan and not quite enough time.
>
> Chinese Proverbs

The ritual is the foundational story and expression of the crafts values, upon which the leader is never to innovate. But as leaders in other situations, when planning the work of the team, you are to be ever vigilant and innovative in assuring that all resources are utilized to their greatest potential and everyone involved understands how important it is for them to deliver their results in a timely manner.

M = Mistakes

> "There are no secrets to success. It is the result of preparation, hard work and learning from failure."
>
> Colin Powell

Our humanity assures that we, our colleagues and peers will make mistakes. Advancement will take place when we study the failures, recognize all or some of its causes, and make advances to reduce the probability of similar conditions leading to the same type of failure.

WISDOM is a natural and important philosophy for leading well.

The 5 W's

Who, What, When, Where, Why.

Leadership involves becoming a good listener and questioner. Particularly when engaged in problem solving or the development of growth initiatives for your organization. Show your passion, your knowledge, your willingness to assist others, and support the goals, interests and plans for the group by asking quality questions to fill in the basics, Who, What, When, Where, and Why.

The 5 W's are what the old school journalist used to test whether they had the major points for a complete story. You can use this to develop a complete understanding of a subject. If, after a discussion you cannot fill in these details, then you need to go back to get more information.

So let's work through the 5 W's

Who?

> Who is involved in the subject at hand? Do you know everyone involved? Who will be present during the discussions? Who has influence or a vested interest in the subject? Knowing the players, supporters and those who are for or against the discussion point is crucial to understanding the big picture.

What?

> Typically, in the discussion of what, the focus is achieving and understanding the facts, but be open to the idea that on certain occasions understanding the emotion, motivation and the history of the subject can be valuable to understanding the full scope of what is involved. At the conclusion of this line of questioning, you should be able to list all of the relevant events or activities of what will happen and what has happened.

When?

> Timing is everything. Knowing when activities will or did happen, and the conditions relevant to the timing. For examples did the event take place during the day or night, was it winter or summer, did it occur before, during or after another event. This context will be important for recognizing how timing will influence the outcome. Your goal is to be able to talk about the sequence of events.

Where?

> Location, location, location, the primary rule of real estate also applies to developing an understanding. Understanding where all parties and components are situated and their relative positions and the context of those positions, is important to know. It adds another layer of detail when discussing events and theories. Knowing where everything should be in order to accomplish meeting an activities can be vital in the successful outcome of your events.

Why?

> The all important "why"? Understanding the conditions that led to a result and what precipitated the actions can be fundamental to understanding.

Understanding who, what, when, where and why, can provide you a fundamental and detailed level of understanding. Upon which you can make well informed decisions or plans.

Setting directions and priorities depends on everyone having a firm grasp on your organizations current and future state. Answering the 5W's in sufficient detail will give you the proper perspective to advance your current state and this will point you in the right direction.

SWOT Analysis

A SWOT analysis is a method for collecting a team's thoughts and documenting the strengths, weaknesses, opportunities, and threats that can help or harm the team's ability to reach their defined objective and goals.

Analyzing internal forces: strengths/weaknesses and external forces: opportunities/threats will assist you in selecting activities that will help you leverage the positives and overcome the negatives that can impact reaching your goals.

The key purpose of the analysis is to tease out the thoughts that will help you to create a roadmap and align the organization's resources while also becoming aware of the potential pitfalls. The SWOT analysis is the foundation for evaluating your potential and limitations. A regular review of your SWOT analysis will become your organizations reference for including these global considerations in day-to-day decision making.

The best way to create a SWOT analysis is to involve the key members of your team in one or more brainstorming sessions. For each S-W-O-T category, create a supporting list of ideas. Next, prioritize the list, ultimately selecting the statements that are truly the most important and have the largest impact. One statement in a category is acceptable, five is a good number, and more than 10 is usually unmanageable and requires refinement. Of course your own good judgment will help you decide the quantity of items to use for your purpose.

Keep your SWOT statements factual and unemotional. For example, instead of stating strength as, "Our service is the best," you might say, "Customers prefer our service because they complete their transactions 50% faster than our biggest competitor."

SWOT

Figure 3: SWOT Template

To produce a SWOT analysis diagram, make a chart with two rows and two columns. Place your chosen strengths in the upper left corner, place weaknesses in the upper right corner, place opportunities in the lower left corner; and finally your threats in the lower right corner. Each category you've placed can support the following questions:

Strength: Strengths are the qualities that enable the organization to accomplish its mission.

- What do we do better than anyone else?
- What is uniquely and authentically us?
- What is our strongest asset?
- What do we do well?
- What else do others see as our strength?

- What do we offer that makes us stand out from others?
- What is unique about us?
- What are the resources we have that add value?

Weakness: Weaknesses are the qualities that can prevent the organization from being its best and may prevent the completion of its mission and priorities.

- What could we improve?
- What do others perform better than us?
- What should we avoid?
- What do others think are our weaknesses?
- Is there a skill or expertise that we that we are missing?
- Are we organized and structured well?
- Are we sufficiently funded, are the finances in order?

Opportunity: Opportunities are presented by the environment within which the organization operates. These arise when an organization can take advantage of conditions around to become more successful.

- What are the trends that can help us or the trends which we can take advantage of?
- What are organizations in similar or different industries doing that we might model?
- What have you seen in the news or read recently that might present an opportunity?
- What are the financial opportunities toward gaining strength?

Threat: Threats arise when conditions in the external world/environment negatively impact the organizations ability to be successful.

- What trends could harm us?
- What difficulties may be in front of us?
- What weaknesses are we seeing in the industry or the market place?
- What do we anticipate the competition will do?
- Do we anticipate any negative financial trends?

With this analysis information, the idea is to focus on your strengths and minimize your weaknesses. You should continue to revisit your SWOT Analysis as things change with time.

This is not an exercise to be performed and put aside. In addition to investing the time to think, you should put actions into place to build upon your strengths, using them to their fullest capability, and plan to reduce the impact and risk of your weaknesses, either by making changes to get rid of them or by reducing their frequency or negative results. In considering your opportunities, with effort you may be able to turn them into valuable assets and generate plans to take advantage of every opportunity you have the resources to exploit. Try to turn threats into opportunities. Attempt to be proactive, and put plans into place to counter any and all threats as they arise.

Chapter Two ~ Fellowcraft

"You're right on time, thanks for coming", said James. He then pulled out his note book, a leather-bound journal with ruled pages and the Square and Compass embossed on the binding. "Have you prepared to answer the standard first question? What have you learned recently in Masonry that aligns with your work experience?"

"I have given it some thought," said Samuel. "My time as a Fellowcraft has made me focus on being a good team player. Let me get my list, from my coat pocket."

Sam, pushes and tapped his Smartphone, "OK, here goes, my list."

1. Study and know the fundamentals.
2. Be friendly.
3. Be collaborative.
4. Be faithful.
5. Be a constructive member of the team.

"So, here is my thought on the first item," he said.

"First, to be a good team member, you must understand your craft and deeply understand the fundamentals of the work. Your competence and ability to positively contribute to the teams efforts is critically important to being successful. If you were an accountant and you were not a detail-oriented person or lacked strong knowledge of the subject, it would be very difficult to be a highly-valued member of the team. The team would be impacted by your incompetents and they would most likely spend non-productive hours fixing what you have not completed. Whatever other asset a person brings to the team, it is hard to get past his incompetence and inability to bring the basics and fundamentals to the table. So focus on knowing your craft."

"Next, the second item on the list, bring the skills necessary to establish a team and/or friendship. You may never get past sharing business information and treating the person across the table from you as an acquaintance, but respecting them as you would a friend is powerful in establishing a respectful relationship. Teams work well when each person is respectful of all of the team members. Teams also work well when everyone is open and listens to and considers the opinions and information shared by all colleagues. In difficult times, teams and friends rally around each other. In positive times friends and teams are happy for you and for the team. Friendships are not always equal in effort, time committed, and strength, but when working correctly, everyone involved is consistent in what they bring to the table and steps up when necessary to support each other in the relationship. In the same way, teams and their members are not equal. Equal is seldom the most efficient or proper way to get things done; however utilizing everyone to the best of their ability, and enabling them to do the things they do well, will bring about a good team dynamic."

"When you find ways to work together, sharing ideas with little concern for credit, finding the synergy in ways that make 1 + 1 greater than 2. Under these conditions, ideas are better and solutions are better. When synergy exists and multiple people are properly engaged in the development and execution of the work product, the outcome will be good."

"These collaborations are most efficient when everyone is a reliable member of the team, when all can be trusted to complete their assigned tasks on time, on budget, with quality, and completely. Then finally, being sensitive to the needs of the team and being supportive and actively participating in the work and output of the team can be the final ingredient in the successful growth of a team."

"My Masonic class and I are working together nicely," Samuel continued. "I was talking to a classmate and he was sharing that while I was away, the rest of the class got together a couple of times to study and really worked with the least proficient member of the class. He said that if I was not careful and did not continue to study, I could become the weak link in the class. I won't let that happen. In fact, we are resolved not to have a weak link among the class. We have all brought sufficient skills and effort to enable us to study as a group and in private. We also have also bonded enough to know we can trust one another to respond to a call for assistance. Our sessions enable a constructive learning environment. We have proven to be dependable, and the constructive feedback and compiling of information have made our learning invaluable. I've been told that back in the day, it was typical for a man to learn this process of becoming a mason alone with no classmates. I'm glad we have changed that practice. Working as a team is much more my style." said George.

"Brother Samuel, you've mentioned that your efforts were hindered because of travel and activities at work. Tell me more about how the team responded and what were your efforts to stay connected?"

"Technology really helped although I couldn't write questions as it is part of the Masonic Code of Conduct not to write down what we study, I found ways to ask questions via private one-on-one conversations and phone calls. I could say things like, "Remember what we talked about last Thursday, before class? I need help remembering what came next." Anyway, my classmates have gotten to know me and with context, could provide me with the one or two words or pieces of information that I needed, to get me right back on track."

"Is the secrecy inhibiting to you?" asked James.

"No. Not really. First, the things that are not shared are not all that foreboding. Second, I can respect the notion that an organization does not share all of its secrets; it is what makes them different. Yet, I also know that even when organizations have their secrets revealed against all of their best efforts, others can't always duplicate their success. It's like my sister trying to make a 7-up cake from the recipe my grandmother gave her. A pinch of this, a dash of that, a cup of another ingredient, were in the recipe she received. When she was finished with her first attempt making the cake, it was a complete flop. So, she made a special trip to my Grandma's with all of the ingredients to watch her make the cake. She learned while watching Grandma mixing the ingredients for the cake, that one person's documented pinch can sometimes be a leveled army spoonful. In the business world corporate culture, values and priorities will make different companies respond to the same stimulus and information differently. Therefore, the outcome can be different even having the same recipe (information)."

"What have you found consistently in your learning so far?" said James.

"Part of advancing the goals and values of masonry are to develop a deep understanding of the tools available to you. Then you must move beyond the practical use of the tools and learn how to interact and control them to achieve different, more creative and greater results."

"Can you extend this concept, for me?" asked James.

"OK, here's an example. A musician is acclaimed for the creativity of their initial work, the use of their instrument in a new and authentic way: be it their voice, a string, a wind, a key or percussion instrument. Then, additional acclaim is given for developing such a high level of skill utilizing their instrument that they can reproduce the initial work in a repeatable way under varying conditions. Whether it is raining or snowing, sunny or cloudy, day or night, indoors or out, the proficient artist can reproduces that their initial creative work, again and again."

"In the Fellowcraft degree," Samuel continues, "there are seven interrelated arts and sciences, each affecting and relating to each other in grand and interesting ways. It is the understanding, utilization and mastery of these arts and sciences that gives inspiration and creativity to the world and its relationships. My class has spent three sessions, so far, learning the importance of the liberal arts and sciences, of which we have been instructed there are seven; grammar, rhetoric, logic, arithmetic, geometry, music and astronomy.

"The seven liberal arts and sciences have been broken into two groups. The first set is related to language and the second set relates to mathematics."

"The first group includes grammar, rhetoric and logic."

"Grammar is that portion of language that permits us to fine tune our verbal and written communications by understanding its structure and rules. It is the art which qualifies us to write and speak correctly, and is enhanced as we increase our vocabulary."

"Rhetoric is the portion of language that allows us to influence others and it promotes the development of methods for communication that will have an impact upon the listener. Think debate team. Rhetoric is the art of using your communication skills effectively in daily life, when influence is required."

"The last and we have been told the most important portion of language is logic, which permits us to think and reason deeply. Logic is the pursuit of understanding, which enables us to correlate information, definitions, and other sources of meaning, so that we can discern right from wrong, and the validity of information. We have been taught the importance of logic is reinforced by the idea that it allows us to understand the duty we owe to God and toward each other."

"Mind you, this is from my notes," Samuel said, as he broke from his notes. "I hope one day to be as fluent as some of our brothers, when discussing masonry. The next group is centered on mathematics and includes arithmetic, geometry, music and astronomy.

"Arithmetic is the method by which we are able to add and divide weights, distances and other measurable items. Arithmetic is the science of calculating all things that are defined by numbers. Without arithmetic many things are inconceivable, unintelligible and/or incomprehensible."

"Geometry is a recognized part of Freemasonry. It is the quintessential science upon which the fraternity is based and is a part of what makes the organization identifiable and unique. Geometry allows us to create right-angles, the symbol of our uprightness and to square our actions in alignment with God, one another and our fellow creatures. Every excellent and well conceived structure can be planned and measured by this science."

"Music is a mystery to many, and its connection to mathematics is an enigma to many more but to anyone who is skilled in the art of creating music, the connection is apparent. Music is the coordination of time, space, sound, amplitude, frequency and pitch, which can all be represented by numbers."

"Astronomy is the art by which we can view the great symmetry of the hand of the deity, according to our teachings," Samuel continued. "Many of our fraternal symbols, the sun, the moon, the stars, are borrowed from the science of astronomy. Astronomy, teaches the laws of the celestial world and its relevance to our terrestrial existence. It is the celestial phenomenon which we study to understand and build upon the natural rhythm and sequence that determines the course of the sun, the regularity of the moon, and the position of the stars. Astronomy allows relevance and consistency for the things that are temporal. In addition, Time is that most precious of commodities. It is the proper utilization of time that is the measure of a life. You may have heard the saying, 'the means justify the extremes.' The teachings of the fraternity are that in business and in the conduct of many other things, you will be judged by their outcomes. But a life, oh, that is an entirely different matter: In life, you are measured by how you lived, the intent of your actions, and your sufficient use of time. It is not the outcome that is of greatest value, for we all start at birth and finish at death. But it is your utilization of the time that really matters, and which is to be judged."

"Freemasons focus on the arts and sciences as a metaphor for the tools to be used and engaged and developed, as a part of a life of self-improvement and personal growth. It adds focus and emphasis to the Masonic goal of taking a good man and making him better."

The point and the alignment with business and masonry that I have made is that there is a lot of work effort required to understand the full depth and breadth of this vast set of subjects. The sheer size supports the notion that there is always more learning for an individual mason. But to optimize the organization, there is a need for specialists and generalist around this vast array of knowledge elements, to bring the organization into balance and to continue to grow the institutional knowledge, understanding, and utilization of these arts and sciences for the betterment of mankind. The same can be said of an organization, there is a need for specialists and generalists, and getting them to perform their roles in a systematic and coordinated fashion will enable growth and the delivery of high quality serve to the customer.

Deeper into Leadership

Here, in this section, we will further the concepts for leaders and Worshipful Masters to utilize while working with their teams and lodges. There will be a few concepts upon which you can focus your attention, as you develop greater interpersonal skills and personal values.

Communications

As a leader it will be critical for you to develop and practice your communication skills. This will be fundamental in the development of your interpersonal skills. For a Worshipful Master of a Masonic Lodge, the expanse of his communication skills should be as boundless as his service to mankind and his willingness to dispense charity. He is entrusted to communicate with the various individuals and groups within the Masonic family including, but not limited to, the Sisters of the Order of Eastern Star, and the leadership and members of other Masonic houses. As a leader he is to be an ambassador of love, support and information for his members. He may be the single best access point for the fraternity and provide a path for the community to formally engage with your lodge resources. In your engagements you should be clear and concise with all requests. You are to read often, the ritual for better consistency and teaching, the constitution and statues for better legislation, Masonic news for better direction and governance, and current events to enable better community service. In your engagements, seek out fresh ideas, updated strategies, as well as cutting edge methods and techniques for better Lodge management.

As a leader, you must communicate within the hierarchy of your organization. Depending on the area of your expertise and the development of your speaking skills, you may be asked to make presentations and/or to represent your lodge and/or organization at public functions. You should lead with dignity and decorum at all proceedings of your lodge and any formal or informal meetings with your organizations members.

Listen intently and carefully to establish good communication. This is the responsibility of all involved, including both senders and receivers. Never take lightly your responsibility to be understood and consider greatly your responsibility to understand the messages of others. As a leader or Worshipful Master you are empowered and entrusted with the wisdom to rule on behalf of your organization. Be sure to guide your group with good input, endeavor to hear all that is shared and endeavor to communicate your decisions clearly for all to understand.

Write often and share it with many. As discussed earlier, you should make known the vision and directions for your lodge and of your organization. Additionally you should make known your calendar of events and the successful results from past enterprises, in your writing.

Speak highly of everyone. Talk of ideas, values, and plans, and speak less of people, especially their foibles.

Your leadership will be judged with great weight placed upon your communication skills. You will be measured on the wisdom contained in your messages, the content of your character, the delivery of your story, and the reception and actions taken by your Brothers, friends, peers and associates. Enhance and develop your communication skills and you will grow as a leader.

Here are a few considerations for improving your communication effectiveness.

Subject Matter Expertise - Focus on the things you do best and continually develop your expertise. Make an effort to learn something new and useful every day to add depth to your understanding and expand the area of your expertise.

Stay Cool – When everyone around you is losing their composure and temperament, stay focused on the job. Don't over-react and do not invest in retaliatory tactics.

Focus – Direct your full attention upon the people with whom you are talking. Put away your Smartphone. Leave that tablet in its case. Look at people directly to let them know they have your complete attention.

La Familia - Within your team and with members of other departments, create mutually beneficial partnerships. Be like a family. A well-functioning family is one in which everyone gets their needs met. Each person may not get everything they want but they get everything they need and equally important everyone should feel heard.

Stay Open-Minded - Work with colleagues, especially during a crisis from the perspective that most problems can only cause a limited amount of damage. The number of solutions for fixing the damage can be unlimited. In a moment of crisis, focus immediately on solving the incident. Later, focus on long-term future problem resolutions, risk mitigations and failure-prevention strategies.

Pride - Imagine every task and project you complete will carry your name and reputation. Zealously guard these and don't lose them because of inappropriate communication or actions.

Utilizing communication effectively can enable a participative style of interaction within the team and with people who are interested can provide many positive benefits. As a leader or Worshipful Master, planning may take more effort and coordination on your part, but the end product will be a more democratic. Once fully realized there is awareness, an investment and a level of positive support that is built around everyone's participation. This will yield a positive team dynamic and an engagement that promotes a wide set of people and team members working toward a common goal they helped to create.

Establishing project controls and directions tends to be easier when everyone involved is engaged and knowledgeable regarding how their work is interrelated and how their work supports a larger vision.

In addition, the delegation of responsibilities becomes easier when there is an open disclosure and discussion of roles and responsibilities. The more people engage in this process and the more input is received, the better the final results. Developing an understanding of what you want delivered and clearly communicating your expectations in a way that is understood by others, is vital to the success of your organization.

Confidence and Enthusiasm

Everyone wants to be confident. It's a concept that is discussed by almost everyone at some time. It is discussed by those who are shy and introverted, and by those who are talented, successful and have plenty of confidence. We're all human and for most of us there are times, places, and occasions when we feel we could use more confidence. For leaders, some occasions may include such situations as presentations, interviews, demonstrations and offer various speaking engagements. We want to perform at our very best in any situations. When under pressure, you may feel you need confidence. Here's a perspective you can use to turn that lack of confidence completely around. Consider what you may need is simply a new perspective, enthusiasm. Here are a few references for how the new perspective and enthusiasm can realign your attitude and in turn your confidence.

If you are focusing on being confident, you are focusing on your needs. This point of view makes getting caught up in self-doubt easier. Your inner voice asks questions like, "Can I do this? Will I be able to get it done?" However when you focus on a topic and your desire to share the information that you have acquired, then focus will to create positive thoughts around your subject and will reduce the focus on you. This shift will be toward the work and more enthusiasm in the effort. When you pay attention to the needs of others and how you can help; be it one person, a roomful of people or a whole auditorium, you worry less about what you are doing and feeling, and more about the topic and the people. The redirection of thought can make you more successful, because your focus is properly on the subject and the customer. Asking yourself instead, "Are they happy? Are they getting what they need?" is a more enlightening and revealing set of questions, and opens the door for you to be enthusiastic about helping them to get what they need.

I recently saw a person giving a presentation and I was impressed with their level of what I perceived to be their confidence. But we didn't connect and their confidence was not infectious. It was not transferable. Confidence can be impressive, but be aware of the kind of impression and connection you are making. When you are enthusiastic, it comes through in your smile. It shows itself in your gestures. It is seen in the way you use words. When you have an internal feeling of enthusiasm for an idea, concept or activity, it is difficult to keep inside. If you're open to opportunities, to share what you believe in, the chances are great that others will open up to your idea, concept or activity. Enthusiasm can be highly contagious.

Having confidence when you know what you're doing and when you know you can do it well is a good thing. There are times and opportunities for this kind of confidence but too much confidence can make you appear rigid and rigidity can be stifling. With enthusiasm, there's always an element of openness and spontaneity that can make you more accepting of the unknown. It is not knowing exactly what you or someone else is going to say next and looking forward to the surprise. This is why many scripted speeches can be less interesting and why the atmosphere of an improvised show can be more electric.

Accounts of the creative process contain lots of stories where images, ideas or words "pop into" someone's head – they have a Eureka moment and, invariably, the subject or concept is one for which the person has great enthusiasm.

When you're enthusiastic, about something important it translates into energy and speaking on a topic becomes more fun. There are few things more enjoyable than talking confidently and enthusiastically about something for which you have fire in your heart. Energy is reflective. When you exhibit passion, it will be returned and will draw passionate people toward you.

How you develop your power going forward depends upon your personality, and not the environment in which you grew up in. For example you may have been told that you were stupid, no good, etc. Don't you believe it! If you were one of many people who grew up under such unfortunate experiences and/or if you have not developed a high level of self-worth for other reasons, now is the time to change and learn confidence and enthusiasm-building techniques that can change your life.

No matter where your starting point is on the enthusiasm and confidence continuum, you can grow your success possibilities when you develop a few specific skills. They'll make you a better person who is more focused, balanced, confident and energetic. Having confidence and enthusiasm is easy when you're armed with the proper knowledge to guide you through the building process:

1. Associate with people whom you admire for their confidence and enthusiasm. The old adage, "You are known by the company you keep," is not just an empty phrase. By associating with enthusiastic and confident people, your own levels will surely be improved.

2. Don't give up. Keep going and try out new versions of enthusiasm even if it seems hard. Persistence often wins while you are trying to develop confidence. Hardships and adversity are components of life that can help strengthen you and prepare you for future successes that are hard-earned and well-deserved.

3. An authentic personality is a must when developing confidence and enthusiasm. If you're a fake, others may become aware and reject the fake part of who you are presenting. Sincerity and an effort to share the best of who you are will win the day.

4. Believe you can develop the power within to be successful at building your confidence and enthusiasm. This means accepting where you are today on the confidence and enthusiasm continuum. Make a conscious and continuous effort to believe in yourself and know it will add value to your life. Draw from your inner strength that is in your life and develop it into a positive personality trait.

5. Take on new challenges with a positive attitude and a smile. If you want to be more confident and enthusiastic, you must work at it constantly. Go to that meeting, party or event you'd rather skip and let others know that you are there to contribute.

To succeed you must want something badly enough to work hard at making it happen. Don't hesitate or give a half-hearted effort in finding ways to increase your confidence and enthusiasm level. You can improve your life and now is the time to start.

Balanced Communications

There is another set of angles regarding the discussion of communications skills. How to express your point of view, In addition how to influence, motivate and inspire a team are very important communication attributes.

Have something to talk about backed by a strong point of view illustrated with facts. Express yourself confidently and know what you are talking about. Let there be no doubt, that you are prepared. Let people know that you are sharing information for their use and your expectations are they will use it for their advancement of the teams' goals and mission.

Getting people to listen to you when you have something powerful to say is partially based on your likability. You must work on establishing rapport to influence some and motivate others. Put time and effort into finding common interests and reasons to work and talk together. Building rapport is also essential inspiring others. The secret of developing rapport is about establishing an agreeable pace. This means mirroring the other person and/or audience. Your job is to find ways to be in tune with people, adapt and find common ground. If a person is having a good day, be bright. If a person is having a bad day, be empathetic. Does the person's language suggest that they are visual? If they say, "I can't see what you mean," then show them and draw a picture. If they are visual, they probably want to see details. If they are kinetic they want tangible objects to feel during your conversation. Walk them through the details, with hand-outs and other items they can touch. There are many types of clues and moods to look for. Is a person or group formal or informal? Are they a risk taker or cautious? Are they deliberate and/or quick in their pace? Observe and adjust to meet people where they are.

To have balanced communication you must be a good and strong listener. Seek to listen for understanding. Throughout your conversations, pay attention and become involved. Observe and interact actively. Seek eye contact, observe body language, and listen to verbal responses from other people. Your goal should be to measure whether everyone involved comprehends what is being discussed. Adjust your gestures, tone, and vocabulary whenever necessary.

Communication does not matter whether you are the initiator in the conversation or if you are the closer. Everyone's job after a conversation is to walk away from the dialogue having an understanding of what is being discussed. It is important to ask clarifying questions. To test and verify the degree of understanding of everyone involved. Questions are helpful for everyone to walk away with a clear mutual understanding of the conversation.

Another tool for balanced communication is to summarize discussions for clarity. Throughout conversations, and definitely at its conclusion, summarize for understanding and the positions that have been discussed throughout the discussion. This will help to avoid confusion. Also, choose your words carefully as words have power.

It has been said that a good leader inspires people to have confidence in the leader; a great leader inspires people to have confidence in themselves. Leadership is about people. It is about inspiring people to be their greatest self for the good of the vision and mission of the team. Use balanced communication skills to help teams and their members to find their greatest selves.

Ethics and Etiquette

As a leader, you should adhere to a solid moral place. Always conduct yourself appropriately and carry yourself with a dignity worthy of respect.

In Masonry, we test the character of men who want to join the organization. The common beliefs in the Supreme Being and faith in life after death, provide a deep understanding and a strong foundation for relationships. These beliefs place a high value on ethical character as well as making good decisions. In business, the foundations may be probably less spiritual but should still engender a strong sense of right and wrong. Working with others you can ease negotiations.

A proper use of the rules of etiquette is an easy and common manner for attempting to judge a man's character. This assessment is built on the assumption that an individual of gentlemanly scholarship has been taught many lessons of right and wrong and good conduct. It is an estimation of whether you have been taught how to hold a knife and fork correctly or pass both the salt and pepper shaker together, when asked for either. These may seem like a rather trivial set of rules and skills but they represent the outcome of a learning environment of a person with a support system. A person who knows these basics, may have also been schooled in dinner conversation, how to behave when in public, how to share, how to respect others, and many other basic etiquette and life lessons.

Business ethics is a code and/or a set of relationship standards to which a business adheres. These codes essentially state what is considered right and what is considered wrong in terms of how the business is conducted in relation to what is best for mankind, the community, the environment, and so on. Business etiquette, is also conducting business affairs in a polite and professional manner.

If a doctor has a delightful bedside manner and his or her social and business etiquette are such that she is well-received at any function and performs well in any situation; that usually is a reflection of good etiquette. However if he or she is billing his or her clients for hours that were not work, then this is not ethical. One can have fantastic etiquette can also have extremely poor ethical behavior. Be aware. In addition, if an employee at a call center is rude to a customer, this may not be considered unethical but it is considered poor business etiquette.

Recognize ethics and etiquette and do your best at both. However, if an occasion calls for you to choose between etiquette and your ethics, choose to be faithful to your ethical standards. Your values or what you consider important as it relates and right and wrong, come first. Knowing and understanding etiquette and its uses can provide for an opportunity to smooth a situation over but should never be at the cost of your ethics and values. Never lose your moral position.

Can a strong ethical base be learned and is it also determined by Nature or Nurture? You got your small ears from your father and your brown eyes from your mother, but where did you get your personality and/or talent for sports? Did you learn these attitudes others and/or from your parents or were these things determined by your genes? It may be easy to see that many physical characteristics are hereditary, but genetic traits are less visible when it comes to intelligence, personality, and/or behavior. The old argument of nature vs. nurture has never really been resolved. No one completely knows how much is determined by DNA or how much is determined by our life experiences. However, we do know that both play a part in the development of character traits.

Some scientists believe that people behave according to their genes. This is known as the "nature" theory of human behavior. Other scientists believe that people think and behave in many ways because of how they've been taught and their environment. This is known as the "nurture" theory of human behavior. Some scientist feel nature will dominate each time and vice versa. Nature endows us with certain abilities and traits and nurture takes these abilities and molds them as we learn and mature for certain. Our efforts are to take what we have unduly been given and then take what we have been taught and combine these things to develop into being a positive adult. As adults, we should continue to develop in the manner that we choose and learn to be better leaders, better organizers, and better individuals.

The development of etiquette skills is the "nurture" component of life. The development of your sense of right and wrong and associated values can be taught, developed, and modified. Often, who you associate with is an influence, and is, one of the values of Masonry and many mentor-based relationships. Being dependable, working hard, and being prepared are all aspects of life you can learn and develop. These character traits regarding ethics and etiquette are not preordained. Developing skills and character traits that help you achieve your goals should be totally in your control.

Project Management Tools

In formal project management, the two words that are most dreaded are "earned value." Earned value is the method of collecting information about the progress of tasks that make up a project and utilizing that information to determine whether the project will be completed early, on time or late and other analysis.

Leaders often must manage money and this management task, like others, requires data and the analysis of that information.

In the for-profit world, leadership must be concerned with providing value to its proprietor, shareholders, board, and/or partners. In the not-for-profit world, leadership must be concerned with properly using the funds received from donors, and whether the money is being properly used in support of the organization's goals.

A balance sheet is one standard tool for leaders to understand how to manage money. Note, when reviewing a balance sheet, a key and bottom- line focus should be on improving Shareholder Value, sometimes this will be listed as Owner or Shareholder Equity. This is a measure of the value of the company that has been retained for the shareholders or those that will share in the profits of the company. As an executive in a company, it is your duty to increase the value of this line on the balance sheet. As an investor, seek out this critically important piece of information to help determine the safety of your investment.

As you develop and grow in leadership, your role and where you exist in the organization will influence the exact depth of your scrutiny of the financials and your level of sensitivity to the variations.

My financial variance rules of thumb:

If you are the leader or treasurer for an organization with revenue less than one million dollars ($1,000,000.00), or hold some role responsible for the day-to-day management of money, you are to care about the integrity surrounding the reporting of every penny. Your role is to be accurate and exact. In a larger organization, your role is still to be exact, but margins of error in the 0.01% range may be reasonable.

If you are a board member, or high-level executive for an agency or organization that has revenue less than one million dollars, I suggest that you are sensitive to line items with variances greater than 0.2%. If the organization has revenue of six hundred thousand dollars ($600,000), you should question any budget line item that is off, either by $1,200. If you are further from the internal working of the group, you can be less sensitive to financial variance, more to the tune of 0.5%. With the same example value of six hundred thousand dollars ($600,000), you may not see red flags and question the finances until the variance is greater than $3,000.

However, this is a guideline, not a rule. In all instances you must be faithful to your fiduciary responsibilities and assist the organization to make good financial decisions and properly report the same.

QCD – Quality, Cost & Delivery
Good, cheap, fast. I'll have one of each, please!

Traditionally, there exists an idea and a project-constraint model which recognizes three key elements that determine the success of a project; "cost," "time" and "quality." Any project or activity, exhibits is a strong relationship between these elements. When there is a requirement to modify any one of these elements. It is assumed that at least one of the other factors may be affected as a result.

Quality

This is the big opportunity for organizations. High-quality outputs usually best leverages the investment made in development. But, if you want good results, you have to prioritize content and requirements. Good results are usually not achieved as a bolt-on (a late addition often attached to the exterior of the product or component and not properly integrated into the product or output). Quality is often best when it is an integral part of the project.

Cost

Working with a client in search of a low price means more stress for less money. My view is that clients who want everything at a discount don't see the output as important to the business. For them, it's more like buying office supplies or insurance. It's a commodity. The perspective you are seeking is a belief that, if something is important, it's worth paying for it to be done properly. Nobody asks for the cheapest brain surgeon.

It is possible to do things efficiently. This is not the same as cheaply, but it can save money. For example, you may save money by resetting a client's expectations about how much work they need to be satisfied. Consider the committee chairman that is planning a journal as a part of the fund raising for an event, and thinks the journal should be one hundred pages, because another lodge had a book that big and his lodge has had a journal approaching one hundred pages for the past few years.

Consider the goal of the journal, the message to be conveyed and the cost that is incurred in the finishing as the number of pages grows. Consider that with, just a little consideration and managing of the expenses, the same financial profit may be achieved and the proper message conveyed properly with only an eighty-five page journal. There would be less work, less cost, and the same results. Success!

Delivery

Most clients have a schedule: a deadline, a business-plan commitment, a product launch, a start date which is very immovable. Consequently, many projects start with time constraints that sometimes leave little opportunity for planning or research as the completion date quickly approaches. You would love to be able to say that "a lack of planning on your part does not constitute an emergency on my part," but it sort of does if the customer is paying for your time!

The best antidote to being pressured for time is to be focused and eliminate mistakes; to be fast, be accurate and plan out the work very carefully to avoid errors. For example, if a task has a window of idle between getting approval and completion, schedule your time during that gap to perform future activities, preliminary work or verify that critical parameters, information or processes are precisely defined and implemented. Re-doing work and problem resolution is time consuming and wasteful, so this is a reminder that an ounce of prevention is worth a pound of cure.

*~

Back in the day we had a saying about project management: 'You can select any two of fast, cheap or good' but you can't have all three. It's a choice that most people don't want to make.

Good + Cheap = Slow

Choose good and cheap, and the team will do a great job for a discounted price; but be patient and wait until they have a free moment between completing priorities and work from clients who are willing to pay a better.

Good + Fast = Expensive

So, you want high quality and you need it quickly. Choose good and fast, and the response is the team will postpone other activity, cancel appointments and stay up extra hours per day just to get your job done. But, don't expect it to be cheap; there is a cost to be paid for receiving priority.

Fast + Cheap = Inferior

Choose fast and cheap, and expect an inferior product delivered on time. You truly get what you pay for, and, in my opinion, this is the least-favorable choice of the three.

Today we believe this to be a slightly false choice, as good planning and execution can yield a rising tide upon which all factors can be raised.

Time Management

A young man asked his elder for the secret to being successful. The older gentleman pondered the question for a moment and then responded, "Be on time." In the past, wise advice was to be 15 minutes early rather than one minute late. The times have changed a little and now there is a concern for being too early. Nonetheless, try to be a little early or on time for everything.

Sage advice, you can be the best of help and you can develop positive relationships and engagements only when you are present. If you can't be present and can't on time, don't accept the role or assignment. If you commit to being somewhere, be there.

From personal and professional relationships, to negotiating the interests of a multi-million dollar business, being true to your word and showing up on time is critical to developing relationships and ultimately to your success. Being late and not showing respect for another person's time may be detrimental, so make people feel that for the time when you are with them they are the most important thing in your world.

A practical suggestion for how to manage your time so that you can get things done and be "on time" is to start your day and/or end your day by writing a "to-do list." The objective is to have a schedule that is full of the right things to do and gives you the time to focus on being on time and being prepared.

A quick process for managing your "to-do list" is to write everything down that you need and want to do, including both short and long term activities. Then ask yourself the following three questions for each item in order to prioritize your list:

1.) Is this important?
2.) Is this urgent?
3.) How much time will this take?

Is this important?

Importance is to be measured relative to your vision for life or the organization's direction. Importance defines the activities that really matters. Sometimes people don't handle the important activities in their lives well, because they give them insufficient time. Also due to the pressures to perform other daily tasks, they may neglect working on the important tasks. So, identify the important activities and make sure you are advancing those things consistently. This is the path to successfully managing your time using your to do list and will help you to stay focused on your priorities. The understanding of importance cannot be under-estimated.

Is this urgent?

Urgent activities demand immediate attention and are often the things on which we most need to concentrate. The consequences of not dealing with them now are usually immediate.

When you don't plan how to invest your time, urgent requests and other interruptions, may overwhelm your day. This can lead to a few of your important tasks not being completed as intended. Your goal is to be responsive and consistently meet deliverables on your "to-do list". A small amount of planning can go a very long way.

How much time will this take?

Estimating time is an art for most of us. Ultimately we all estimate time, although some of use estimate tasks in a much less structured and more intuitive way. Consider what you know about the task, add your personal experience or the way you have seen others handle a similar task and estimate how long the task will take.

With a list of tasks, importance, urgency and time-estimated assignments written down, the next thing to do is to prioritize which tasks you should work on first.

The Importance/Urgency matrix tool can be used to organize this prioritization step, especially when working in a group. The Importance/Urgency matrix is a visual aid that can add context to making decisions about getting things done.

Here is a description of how the matrix looks and its use:

In a 2x2 matrix: there should be two rows and two columns

The top row is for tasks you identified as important. The bottom row is for items which are less important.

The first column is for non urgent tasks and the second column is for urgent tasks.

With this setup, the top right section will contain items that are both important and urgent.

Now, write your tasks into their assigned sections based on your input for importance and urgency.

Here is, in reverse order, for the way to handle each quadrant in the matrix:

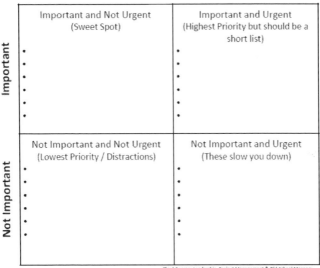

Importance/Urgency Matrix

Figure 4: Importance/Urgency Matrix

Not Important and Not Urgent (Bottom Row / First Column)

These are generally distractions to you and should be avoided if at all possible. If you are clear about your goals, your boundaries and your focus, people will less frequently ask you to perform unimportant activities. If these types of tasks do make it to your list, try to get it reassigned to someone whose goals may be more aligned to the task or only work on it when all other things are done or in a wait state.

Not Important and Urgent (Bottom Row / Second Column)

These items slow you down from achieving your goals, and can keep you from completing your priority work. A common source for tasks in this quadrant is the natural interactions you have during the day, including phone calls, hallway meetings, email and conversations over food. Be confident enough to say, "No," when you are asked to accept a task that you do not believe is appropriate or necessary. Don't be afraid to let people solve their own problems, and don't let them give you their problems unwarranted.

Another strategy is to allocate time for handling interruptions. Consider having a regular meeting to discuss problems or only receiving (answering) calls during specific times in your day.

The objective is to focus on the higher, more important activities, for larger chunks of time.

Important but Not Urgent (Top Row / First Column)

Here is the sweet spot of tasks. When you are working on these tasks, you are managing your time, doing the right things and not letting things get out of control. Do what you can to make sure you have plenty of time to do these tasks. It will enable you to grow in your personal, professional and Masonic life.

One additional special consideration for working in this space is to not let the "not urgent" become "urgent," so take a second look at the expected completion dates for these tasks and avoid letting them become urgent because of neglect.

Urgent and Important (Top Row / Second Column)

When things are in this quadrant, they are the high-priority activities for the moment.

You don't want a lot of tasks in this category, but when they make it to this category; they are worth your focus and attention. In your attempt to manage this category, consider how this task got into this quadrant, and maybe will be things you can do to prevent the pressure and stress related to the urgency of the task. If you are struggling with procrastination, and that is the cause for a task to migrate to the urgent category, hopefully using this tool and paying attention to pending deadlines will help to reduce the frequency of tasks left to the last minute.

The objective is to work on the life-affirming things, and not let the noise of life become too overwhelming, thus preventing you from the important things you want to achieve in your service to God, your neighbors, your family and your well-being.

SIPOC

SIPOC, is a tool used to review and focus on a process or a step in a process and enables a discussion for making the process better.

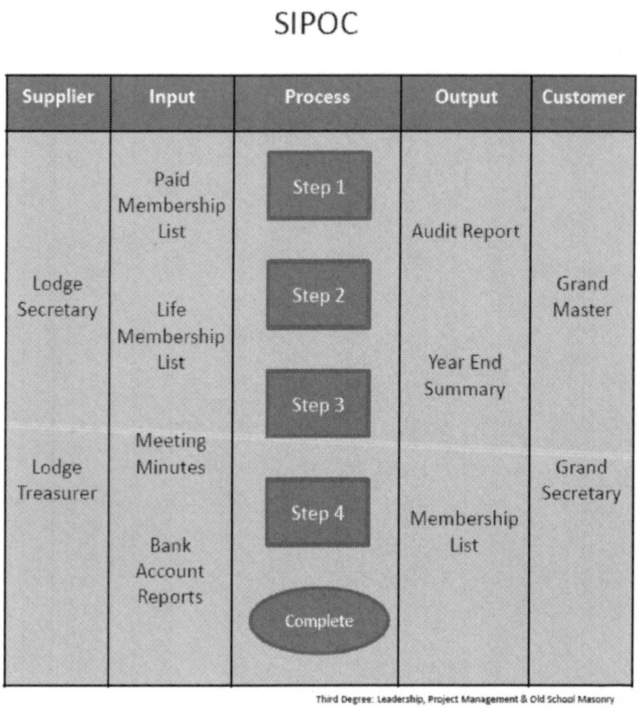

SIPOC

Supplier	Input	Process	Output	Customer
	Paid Membership List	Step 1	Audit Report	
Lodge Secretary	Life Membership List	Step 2		Grand Master
		Step 3	Year End Summary	
Lodge Treasurer	Meeting Minutes	Step 4		Grand Secretary
	Bank Account Reports		Membership List	
		Complete		

Third Degree: Leadership, Project Management & Old School Masonry

Figure 5: SIPOC representation diagram

The five letters stand for:

S = Supplier, I= Input, P= Process, O = Output, C = Customers.

Suppliers are the individuals and/or groups who provide input to the process being discussed.

Inputs are specific content received from the supplier.

Process is usually drawn as flowchart, but can also be written as a description for the process.

Outputs are the information, energy, or tangible items produced by the process.

Customers are the consumers and users of the outputs.

The heart of a SIPOC diagram is a representation of the process. Most people like to see the process in a flow chart primarily constructed through the representation of three types of actions.

- Process steps - a description of the work that is performed.
- Decisions – the representation of the questions asked during the process. Usually these questions result in a "yes" or "no," or a "true" or "false" result.
- Final dispositions – this represents the final tasks that yield an output that can be passed on to the customer or becomes the input for another process.

With the process documented the next step when looking at process improvement is to review the inputs, outputs and people involved in their creation and usage.

Your review of the SIPOC may enable you to lower the risk in the process being reviewed or improve its efficiency. If you talk to the people involved, and solidify an understanding of the 5W's (Who, What, When, Where, Why) and How, you may be able to improve to quality of the inputs and outputs so that you have a better chance of creating a successful process.

Prevent the Garbage in – Garbage out syndrome: Most processes can't succeed without quality inputs or they run inefficiently because they invest a lot of energy in searching for and correcting poor quality input. On the other side of the equation, you should validate that your outputs meet the needs of each and every one of your customers.

Finding efficiency or improved quality in a process, especially in a process that has existed for a long time can take extra effort, but success will yield benefits if it is a process that is used frequently or handles things that are critical to the business.

More time-management ideas:

Divide big things into manageable chunks, and then decide what part you will accomplish next. James shared this story: "My aunt died several months ago and I was assigned as executor of her estate. I had 45 boxes of unidentified and undocumented items delivered to my home. The boxes took up an entire wall of the garage, and I had to sort through all of them. At first I was overwhelmed by the thought of going through all those boxes, but after three months of procrastination, I committed to filing or discarding at least one box a week. Thinking about one box at a time was achievable, also seeing the pile shrink each week was motivating. Forty-five boxes was an overwhelming thought but one box at a time was manageable. The smaller chunks helped me to get through the process."

Another trick for avoiding procrastination is to pick the right time to take a break. The concept is not to stop until you are on a roll. I make sure that, when you pause, you know what you want to write next—so getting restarted is a little bit easier. If, you take a break when you have finished a complete idea, You will have to start fresh next time, which now includes figuring out what to write next. Stopping your work at a place that makes restarting easy is motivating and has a positive impact on efforts that require development over a long period of time.

Stakeholder Analysis

A brief definition of a stakeholder is anyone who is effected by or has an interest in the project and/or its inputs and outputs. This can encompass a broad array of people. For example, it may include senior leadership, internal and external customers, auxiliary organizations, customers of your customers, vendors, contractors and team members.

Part of the role of a project manager is to help an organization understand the depth, breadth and scope of the requirements that are being discussed. One important task is to clarify the scope of the project and assure the needs of the stakeholders are satisfied. Gaining the right perspective is sometimes accomplished through a stakeholder analysis, which, at its essence, is an effort to talk to everyone involved with the project, and to review the projects inputs and outputs, all in an effort to understand the stakeholder requirements, goals and desires of the project.

Stakeholder objectives and requirements should be written in a SMART way, which is a mnemonic for: specific, measurable, attainable, relevant, and time-bound.

Specific requirements should be as detailed as possible. A requirement that is specific will answer some or all of the 5W's (Who, What, When, Where, Why).

Measurable data and/or results are important because when requirements are measurable, we have concrete criteria for measuring the progress of a project, and we have a better chance of satisfying the needs of the business and/or customer. A goal that is measurable will answer one or more of the following: How much, how many, and/or how will I know it's completed?

Attainable goals are defined by simple tests to validate that the requirements of the project not extreme. Requirements may stretch the team but should not be unachievable. An attainable goal is one where someone can answer "How can this goal be accomplished within the time frame and budget of this project?" It does not have to be the final solution; it just needs to pass the test at the moment.

Relevance asks, "Does the requirement matter." Is the requirement important to any of the stakeholders? Is it consistent with the goals and vision? A relevant direction supported by relevant requirements, helps to keep the project focused and this may also help to get the project the resources is needs or the support of senior leaders. Support is hard to achieve if the project and its requirements are not relevant to the decision makers. Relevant requirements answer these types of questions, "Does this goal seem worthwhile? Is this the right time to execute this project? Does this project align with our mission statement?"

Time Bound, is a commitment to a deadline. It is a statement that says the team will focus their resources on the completion of the goal can be achieved on or before the date it is due. A time-bound goal is intended to establish a sense of urgency and to prevent a deliverable from becoming late. A time-bound goal will answer, "When can this be done, today, tomorrow, four weeks, or four months from now?"

Leadership should be guided by the SMART requirements captured during the Stakeholder Analysis. These analysis and the understanding gained from the analysis should enable the team to improve their work process, money management, data collection, and their resource utilization, because they understand the collective needs of the Stakeholders. The Stakeholder Analysis should enable the prioritization of tasks and the proper monitoring of the inputs and outputs of the project.

Chapter Two - Fellowcraft

Chapter Three ~ Master Mason

"Hello, again, my brother!" said James.

"Hello, Brother James, glad to once again be in your company. This time, as a Master Mason in the craft! Wow, that membership process was nothing like I expected. Not that I knew what to expect, but I could not have anticipated what took place. The craft was so well prepared, and I am once again impressed at how much the Brothers can recite from memory. Reciting from memory is truly not one of my personal strengths."

Brother Gordon paused, leafed through a pile of papers, pulled out one, and, in an exaggerated and playful manner, slapped it on the desk with the palm of his hand. "I came prepared to start with the five areas that are in alignment professionally and as a Mason" he said. "After some thought, I believe these items add to how the process made plain the rough parts of the person that I am and gave me the focus to make me better than when I started. I look forward to further developing who I am, and where and how I fit with my classmates, and all the Brothers of the craft. As we can become one common mass, more forceful together than apart and yet each of us internally focused on making sure we keep ourselves intact and don't represent a weak stone in the edifice we are building."

So the five areas are:

1. Personal discipline.
2. Be attentive.

3. Take initiative.
4. Be self-assured.
5. Be your best.

"An interesting list as usual," said Brother James. "Give me a second to write the list in my journal. Ok, Brother Gordon, please share your thoughts behind each of the items."

"First, in my opinion, personal discipline is about getting up every day and doing what is right and what is necessary for you," said Samuel. "It is about focusing on the rules of life that are authentic to you. It is knowing and planning if today is a day where you need peace and quiet or if today is a day where you need to advance your personal mission statement, or to invest in service to your community. Maybe you might perform the paperwork to give a promotion to a team member or visit a lodge brother to study the ritual. It takes a certain discipline to manage and maintain all of the necessities in your life and to drive some portion of your effort toward future success," he continued. "Here are a few areas that you can develop, plan and execute in support of your continued education and personal growth:

Diligently manage your health, take necessary medications, know and maintain your vitals, like blood pressure, sugar levels and weight. Exercise for 60 minutes at least three times a week.

Pay heed to your finances by focusing on your net worth and not on your income or cash flow. This means being sure that you are investing a portion of your money into things that will have enduring value. Also, try not to create debt by purchasing the most recent gadget or toy. I'm not saying you should not purchase things that make you happy or find entertaining ways to spend your time and money on, but finding balance and maintaining the personal sacrifice necessary to grow your long-term personal value is critical in the equation of having a balanced life.

Take care of your body. Be sure to comb your hair, brush your teeth, trim your nails and wash your face. Dress for success. Eat well to take care of your health. The more fruits and vegetables you eat the greater the potential for good health. Drink plenty of water. Finally, in pursuit of your best physical self, get enough sleep. Know your body, mind, and soul."

"Second, there is 'being attentive' to your place on this earth, which is another way of saying pay attention to your surroundings," said Samuel. "Enjoy the arts, music, painting, dance and other creative endeavors. Pay attention to current events and learn things about politics and other news. As a Mason, politics is a taboo subject within the walls of the Lodge room, but as a citizen, do as the bumper sticker says, 'Think globally and act locally.'"

"Being attentive involves being aware of the details in your surroundings and activities. Noticing details can be instrumental in repeating successes and avoiding failures. Details are important when understanding context. Furthermore, focusing on details must be done in a way that enables you to see the forest and the trees. You should always reference the big picture such as your mission and vision. You should frequently adjust your focus and perspective to adjust your activities as well as your short and long term goals."

"The third item, taking initiative, is about not letting life just happen to you. It's about putting your efforts into advancing your life by the way you invest your time, blood, sweat and energy. We have all been given a gift, the gift of life. Don't let your time here in this universe be measured primarily by your inactivity and laziness but rather by your work effort and the wise investment of your personal resources. Do not let the opportunity pass to improve yourself or life that is around you because you did not give it your all. You must always try your hardest when the effort is in true alignment with who you are and who you want to be in the future. To use a baseball analogy, don't watch the pitch go by when it's your turn at bat and the ball is entering the strike zone, give it the best swing you can. Take the initiative to get a hit."

"Fourth, being self-assured is the outcome of positive results from your investment and preparation in your future. When you are prepared, you can be self-assured. However, this does not always translate into being calm, cool and collected. In fact, even with your preparation, there can be an adrenaline rush that makes you feel anxious. Don't let that anxiety take away from the enthusiasm and self-assuredness of your preparation or the idea that you have every reason to feel good."

"For the fifth and final item on the list, your ultimate goal is to be the best person you can be. Your objective should be to focus your energies into making good life choices based on a positive opinion of yourself and a set of values that represent your greatest self. Remain cognizant of the values you have developed through your selection of good role models and mentors; always hearing and considering the wisdom of your elders and those who are subject matter experts. Never become stagnant, recognizing that life is ever-evolving and that your role in this life is to constantly observe your place in this world, to know with conviction who you are and to flow with that conviction to the benefit of mankind. Be true to your inner strength, true to your inner sense of right and wrong, and give the best you have to offer in all that you do. Strive for excellence."

Samuel continues, "There are successes to be achieved. There are mistakes to be made. There are tears, smiles and laughter to be brought forth from you and because of you. As you engage external and environmental conditions you can't control, do your best to manage you and your reactions. The five items are very personal and inwardly-focused, as we use the tools provided to break off the rough parts of who we are to be better fit for the work we need to perform." said Samuel.

"Brother Samuel, that was perfect! Do you have any other thoughts?" asked James.

"My brother, here is a little something that has become clearer because of my participation in Masonry. One of the brothers brought to my mind, an explanation for the phrase, 'giving someone the third degree.' I was told that I would not just be given the third degree (in Masonry), but that I could earn the Third Degree. I asked how I could earn the degree, and the look in his eye and my recollection of the meaning of the phrase quickly gave me the answer. It was just what the commonly used phrase refers to; it is achieved via an intense questions and answers process. It makes me smile to remember the time and effort I spent in preparing for the third degree. It was very satisfying to successfully handle the questions asked of me. As I mentioned earlier, asking good questions can be an important and tangible tool for a leader. Masonry, when executed well, provides a teachable moment and experience, based on the methods and practices of asking good questions and the skill for properly answering."

"Our ancient brethren utilized a strong grilling of men as they entered the organization as the method for assuring the nature of a man's identity, his background and motives. This was achieved through asking thoughtful questions and the assessment of his responses. Today, we have more tools for understanding a man and his background but few tools will reveal his heart the way his efforts for learning our questions and answers, and his interaction with the men of the lodge, will show.

Deeper into Leadership

Here we will take a deeper look into the details associated with leading others and getting things done.

It has been said that "leadership cannot really be taught. It can only be learned." Those words were spoken by Harold S. Green, the leader of ITT at the time. This statement supports my contention that an individual with an aptitude and a willingness to learn can develop good leadership skills but leadership skills cannot be pushed into an individual.

A few additional quotes that point to the perspective that leadership can be learned.

> "If I have the belief that I can do it, I will surely acquire the capacity to do it, even if I may not have it at the beginning." - Mahatma Gandhi

> "Success is to be measured not so much by the position that one has reached in life as by the obstacles which have been overcome while trying to succeed." - Booker T. Washington

> "The leadership instinct you are born with is the backbone. You develop the funny bone and the wishbone that go with it." - Elaine Agather

"If your actions inspire others to dream more, learn more, do more and become more, you are a leader." — John Quincy Adams

Masonry has found a natural progression of responsibilities that help to teach good leadership skills, while also providing opportunities to lead. My Grand Master (which is the leader of masons in a state or jurisdiction) asked me a profound question when I shared that I was writing this book, He asked, "Can you teach leadership?" My answer is I don't believe a person can be forced or taught the knowledge of leadership if they are not in the proper position to receive it. Dwight D. Eisenhower said "Pull the string, and it will follow wherever you wish. Push it, and it will go nowhere at all." But here what I do believe and why I believe this book will be valuable. Whether someone is a leader at all is controlled by having the position or authority to be a leader which is granted by a group or individual when they give you the opportunity to lead. Being given the opportunity to leader is half of the equation, but does little to make you a good or bad leader. Being a good leader rather than a poor leader is 40 percent (40%) controlled by correctly utilizing good leadership skills. The other 10 percent (10%) of being a good leader is being in a position in your life where circumstances and priorities enable you to invest in and make the most of an opportunity granted. This book is primarily about the 40 percent and your investment in preparing to be a good leader and understanding the mechanics of good leadership. It is not easy to be a good leader, but if you are granted the opportunity to lead and you want success for the team, then good leadership skills are the single most important factor in guiding the success of a team.

Before furthering the discussing let's consider in a little more detail the opportunity to lead. Many of us have heard the phrase, "She was born to lead," or "He had leadership thrust upon him." For the most part, when these phrases are used, they are discussions of how the opportunity to lead was achieved. People who are born possibly have leadership opportunities given to them because of a birthright. Their parents may have had money or influence that gave them the opportunity to be in a leadership position. Also, others may have had people in their lives that recognized opportunities for them to lead and steered them in the direction to take advantage of those opportunity. Still other people have leadership opportunities placed squarely in front of them or they are compelled to lead. Further, situations of disaster or intense need, can often bring leaders to the forefront. When there is a lack of resources and/or the need for survival, decisions need to be made quickly. Usually a natural selection process takes place where those that are most creative and willing to express ideas position themselves to lead - especially if others concurred. Under most circumstances many will reach their leadership roles through hard work and some expected and unexpected opportunities to advance and gain leadership skills and experiences. Many may reach leadership roles through the successful execution of minor roles in your leadership ascent. The opportunity to lead is only a partial step to being a good leader.

For most there are no shortcuts to developing successful leadership skills that will make you a good leader. For most must follow and invest in the 10 year / 10,000 hour practice for developing a high level of expertise. The rule states that to develop a high level subject matter expertise, you need to invest 20 hours a week for 10 years, to become one of the best. Starting early helps, but you can always decide to begin your leadership expertise investment at any point in your life. It takes effort, focus, determination and perseverance to achieve leadership skill excellence. Here is an interesting model for thinking about how you can develop leadership opportunities to investing is leadership excellence.

A modern-day educator developed and documented a structured leadership development process that enables her students to see opportunities and take on leadership roles. The process that follows, is abstracted from Kiran Bir Sethi, Founder/Director of the Riverside School in Ahmedabad, India.

According to Sethi, there is a natural progression of leadership that can be taught. In her school, she enables students to progress through three steps which propel them on a journey towards leadership.

Step one - the school teaches the students how to become aware by creating opportunities for the children to see the potential for change. Your role in developing leadership in yourself and/or in others is to see the opportunities for change in the world. Conceiving change is the spark for establishing vision, hopefully with tangible results. Learn to become a visionary.

Step two - the school provides students with opportunities to execute changes by providing practical learning experiences. Your path in developing leadership will also include supporting changes which will yield successes and failures, as both are valuable and an acceptable outcome as learning is the major objective. With successes, challenge yourself and others developing leader skills to be thoughtful and articulate regarding why the tactics used were successful. With failures, take the time to confront the issues of what may have been missed and/or what could have been done better and differently to produce a more positive result.

Step three - the school provides opportunities for students to share their vision. Your objective is to create, share and provide opportunities, for empowering others to embrace change and to invest in a vision.

The attainment of the skills associated with these three steps is the foundation for leadership. Internalize these three steps and remembering how each one will position you for leadership.

As for the last 10 percent associated with good leadership, 'being in a position where life's circumstances enable you to grab opportunities.' Sometimes having an opportunity and skills are not enough to be a good leader. Even if the events in life have given you a rank and title of a leader. Even if you have the knowledge to be a great leader, it will still take your time, energy and often other resources to properly take advantage of what is before you in order to lead well. Sometimes an illness, yours or a loved one's, will change your life's priorities. Sometimes a disaster, that in one instance can propel someone to a leadership role, can also change someone's priorities so that they can no longer or will no longer, take the mantle of leadership. If life circumstances prevent you from executing your leadership skills then your leadership may be in title only.

So, can leadership be taught? Not entirely, but good leadership skills can be taught,

Execution

As a Worshipful Master and leader of masons it is important to work on keeping things moving and in balance. Balanced goals for the organization are relative to the physical, spiritual and emotional needs of those you represent. Always keep learning and focusing on your areas of expertise, by spending 80 percent of your effort growing and sharpening that expertise. Use the remaining 20 percent of your effort to grow the bounds of your knowledge and take opportunities to develop new and innovative ways of learning by attaining greater information from viewing the world in unique ways. Your consistency and fidelity in the execution of your work for the lodge is important to its progress and the advancement of its members.

Being an effective leader sometimes means getting down and dirty. Make an effort to interact with the output of the team. Provide encouragement by demonstrating trust in the organization and its personnel and their ability to produce results. Demonstrating your support verbally, in writing and in your actions can strengthen a team's resolve. Help the team to discover where they need to go instead of telling them the way to go.

It follows the old adage, give a man a fish and he eats for a day, but teach a man to fish and he eats for a lifetime. Showing your trust in your brothers will allow them to make decisions and take initiative, rather than waiting for explicit directions.

Many times your influence will be felt best at the point of problem resolution. Your ability to be a role model regarding these decision making behaviors will be valuable toward enabling the organization's effectiveness.

The Worshipful Masters role in problem resolution is a little unique relative to many organizations mostly because masonry is such a flat organization and the Worshipful Master is the decision authority for most activities. In organizations which have a deeper hierarchy, the higher you are in the organization the smaller the amount of time you spend on the day-to-day activities of the group and the more time you should spend considering the future of the organization, its strategies and the long-term impacts of decisions and investments that will and are being made by your organization.

When you are leading an organization, be very attentive to the messages that are being communicated. When a team is properly engaged, they are hoping for your success as well as their own. They will often give you advice, information and insights. Be aware of the nuances in people's messages, as sometimes people are not direct when speaking with people in leadership positions. You can't and shouldn't heed all of their messages, but the person sharing the message should always leave your encounter feeling heard and believe that you will consider their information. Your willingness to listen to others will strengthen your acceptance from others who will be open to your ideas and opinions. This will foster a safe environment for people to share their ideas and will also allow you the opportunities to make decisions by being well-informed. Good leaders are people that naturally or through the effort of practice listen well and take that ability to engage others so that they see what the leader sees and they believe what the leader believes and are thus inspired by the vision of the leader.

Lastly, be sure to allocate work appropriately to foster greater success in your organization. Provide stretch tasks and provide support. Provide resources to improve chances for success. Turn failed tasks into learning opportunities. Talk about them and don't dismiss them. Also, realize that some casual concerns and questions can generate a lot of unintended activities in the organization so be careful.

Integration

An incremental role of a leader is to get the resources and information necessary to move an activity along. A Worshipful Masters and other leaders must be concerned with the interactions, dependencies and interactions of all aspects of their endeavors. When pulling together their trestle board and other planned activities, it is important to visualize the interconnection of the work. Understanding what activities must occur in what sequence, are important constructs for planning and problem-solving. When considering efficiency, it is important to be sure there are not unnecessary delays in resource utilization. Understanding the dependencies of people and the resources that need to be utilized to complete tasks can prevent conflicts from arising.

Recognizing task conflicts can often be achieved with good planning documentation. Conflicts can be made visible with an integrated plan document, which shows the work tasks, their planned start and finish times and when kept at a very detailed level includes the interrelationship and dependencies between tasks. So, if you can't start one activity before another finishes, this information which is important to good planning, will be made visible. Understanding interdependencies can enable you to release the people and resources to perform other activities rather than becoming idle and waiting. Poorly managed plans can have people and or resources waiting, because none or some of the necessary components are not available to complete the assigned task. Your objective in creating an integrated plan is to prevent the unnecessary waste of resources and to assure that all work activities are thought out. Very detailed tools such as Pert Charts or Microsoft Project should only be used when the detail makes sense. Sometimes a calendar with notes will be sufficient or just a list of work to be done. The important thing is to develop a feel and understanding of the interdependencies that are required for the integration of your work activities.

An additional consideration when developing an integrated plan is to put effort in to improving the efficiency of the organization. When integrating multiple work activities, don't only focus on trying to do more work with fewer resources. Consider the goals of the activity and focus on doing less of the wrong work by putting your planning efforts into eliminating unnecessary and low-value work. Staying focused on the goals of the organization and minimizing activities that don't support the goal can improve efficiency.

A relatively small amount of planning and consideration of the integration of resources, can allow you to utilize your money, people and other resources in the most efficient manner, so that you can be successful for longer period of time and/or with better results. Integrated planning is a good investment.

Innovation and Managing Change

To be relevant tomorrow it is important to project what changes will be required to move from where you are today and closer to what you hope to be in the future. The goal is to estimate where your customers' needs will be in the future, to conceive what you can provide to be of assistance to your customers and identify what investments you can make in the near term so that you can provide pertinent support to your customers in the future.

Innovation is the act of introducing change to achieve something new. Leadership must endeavor to create an environment where the organization seeks to locate opportunities to change and improve processes, products and services, so that they can be better. Some changes are difficult and complex, others are easy and readily achievable and both types of change need to be embraced and are considered valuable. Every improvement does not need to be monumental to be innovative; many times incremental growth is the preferred path for making systemic changes to an organization. Your future as an organization can be bound to your ability to innovate and your ability to move the organization on a path that is consistent with the future needs of your customers.

To manage the type of change that supports organizational growth you must work to balance keeping current customers satisfied, investing in the needs of new markets and potential customers, while supporting internal growth through continuous learning, growing diversity of thought, personnel and opinion, and developing organizational agility. To do this, you need to work with people who bring their whole selves to the work effort of the team. At some level, you need everyone working on the growth of the organization to have a deep commitment to the task and to understand the vision for the future, so that collectively the complexity and dynamics of the community that is a team can work toward a common goal.

Managing change at a cognitive level requires establishing a baseline of understanding, so everyone can visualize a change. The more detailed and vivid the teams understanding of the current state the greater their ability to perceiving a change. Be cautious of focusing too much time on defining the details of the current state, for this can hinder progress and in essences hinder change.

As a leader some consideration should be given to understanding the impact of changes with a clear view on determining if an organizational transformation is required to support a change. Are new committees required or new roles or new positions, necessary to support the change? The inverse can also be true; you may need to eliminate some things to be consistent with the change. Old structures sometimes are inadequate to support a new change. Keeping the team structure optimized is an important role for a leader.

As a team member your effort should validate the alignment of your work and the organizational vision. As the organization evolves and changes around you, you can be vigilant not to stray from the path that was collectively agreed upon, without first getting direction from the creators and maintainers of the vision. You have the responsibility to bring to their attention even the smallest deviation and enable them to reconcile the support or discontinuance of your work if it impacts the organizational vision.

As we all know, change can be difficult. But if a team works together and changes in unison like a flock of birds, then continued and long term success can be the result.

Emotional Intelligence

Emotional Intelligence is an understanding of a person's ability to control their emotions and to sense, understand, and react to other people's emotions in a way that manages to focus on maintaining relationships.

Emotional intelligence has a lot to do with your perception of the world and your place in the world. Also the ability to be self-aware and to regulate one's self has a lot to do with increasing your emotional intelligence. Your understanding and productive use of emotions in social settings will enhance your emotional intelligence. Your ability to manage of emotions, which can be expressed in your ability to show grace, enthusiasm, empathy and genuine concern for the well-being of others, are all indicators of emotional intelligence.

There are studies that demonstrate employer's value emotional intelligence over IQ, because it improves the harmony of the team and enables better collaboration. Given a choice, a manager is more likely to promote someone with high emotional intelligence over someone with a high IQ. In the long run, team cohesion is better served by the person with Emotional Intelligence.

So, how do you know emotional intelligence when you see it? Look for these traits (behaviors and qualities):

- Someone who admits and learns from their mistakes.
- Someone who keeps emotions in check and has thoughtful discussions on tough issues.
- Someone who listens as much or more than they talk.
- Someone who takes and gives criticism well.
- Someone who shows grace under pressure.
- Someone who is empathetic to team members and colleagues.
- Someone who resolves conflict effectively.
- Someone who puts others at ease.
- Someone who leads by example.

An emotionally intelligent person makes a good leader, and usually has the added benefit of being cool under pressure. Learn to develop your personal well-being and be concerned for the well-being of others. Be prepared to take on pressure-filled situations, knowing that with planning and foresight, you can make the situation more manageable. Yet, even in the event of a surprise, keep your wits about yourself and focusing on the problem, and its solution. In addition, show your emotional intelligence by assuring that you maintain and growing the relationships with the people involved.

Project Management Tools

Often organizations and companies handle their most visible concerns the most efficiently. With all of the activities being handled simultaneously in an organization, it is the activities that get monitored and reported in a public way that often gets the most attention. The risk/reward of public visibility is a great motivator. This does not mean that setting up a big brother approach to monitoring the team will resolve all situations nor is setting up mass monitoring programs the right way to make improvements. However there are 2 ways to address organizational efficiency. Do create visible monitoring of critical activities and also communicate a standard of excellence for all activities. More to the first point, if an organization puts forth an effort to monitor metrics on a regular and consistent basis, good things can follow. An organization will naturally adjust and react to changes in a metric. Teams will do things like setting acceptable targets. They will establish ownership for the achievement of metrics. They will debate the organization's capability to impact the metric and the interaction of related activities and variables. There will be a greater effort to develop and implement the right actions to positively impact the metrics being viewed. An organization will naturally correct metrics when they are not trending or meeting their expectations. In meetings and/or forums, the several people present will often provide input and ideas for solutions of the problems. During day-to-day activities, team members will individually consider the impact of their actions and how they influence the metrics that will be used to judge the success of their efforts. Therefore, the monitoring process opens the organization to many positive ways to manage, maintain, and control the metrics. Typically team members will make it a point to prevent bad news and will respond with aggressive action to negate publicity.

Effective Meeting Management

The great resource and common denominator for everyone is time. This makes meeting management an imperative project management tool. The great opportunity we strive for by hosting and participating in meetings is the synergy that can come from the collaboration achieved in a well run meeting. Leadership is a collaborative experience and great leaders know the power and value of a shared experience. The greater good for the organization is achieved when team members have consistent information. The great risk, and time-waster for an organization, is a poorly conducted meeting, where important information is not shared and critical decisions are not made.

A great meeting doesn't just happen. It is usually carefully choreographed, executed by a skilled facilitator, and enhanced by well-prepared participants. Consistently start meetings on time. This indicates that you are serious about time management. It also does not penalize the people who do show up at the appointed meeting start time. An idea supported by research shows that setting a meeting time that is not on the hour or half hour, is more likely to result in people showing up on time. For instance, setting the meeting start time to be

1:05 p.m. rather than 1:00 p.m. will, because of its uniqueness get people's attention; and it should get them to focus on the start time and arriving on time.

When creating an agenda, be sure to set time limits for each topic and stick to that time limit. If you have reach a time limit, the facilitator can consciously and with everyone present understanding the options, to defer the remainder of the conversation to the next meeting or make the decision that this topic is important, which warrants an adjustment to the remainder of the agenda, and/or extending the meeting.

In addition, when setting an agenda, be specific about the outcome desired for each topic being discussed or presented. Is the item on the agenda for the purpose of sharing information and therefore no action is required or is it to make a decision? Is it to work on completing a deliverable? Also, making everyone aware of the intent of the topic allows the team to be focused and prepared. This effort of determining expected outcomes, works best when the agenda, background material and desired outcomes are shared with the meeting participants in advance of the meeting, so that people attending can, and do, come prepared.

A final aspect of effective meeting management is the establishment of ground rules for managing time during the meeting. You may establish rules that prevent an individual from monopolizing a conversation by limiting the number of times an individual can speak on a topic or you can limit the total length of time anyone can speak on a topic. Enforced time limits can help the organization obtain more concise information as the presenters gets better about preparing statements.

When the preparation is right, participants in a meeting can handle their roles. The collaboration that is sought in a good meeting can happen and progress can be made toward achieving the goals of the team. Ultimately, after a good meeting, participants will walk away with better information, a sense of accomplishment and a direction for continuing the effort.

The Pareto Chart

The Pareto Chart is another quality-management tool, primarily used during the early stages of a project, It is designed to help set priorities among a group of activities or when deciding what to focus team efforts on when trying to resolve multiple problems. It can also be used to present data for monitoring a project or activity.

Vilfredo Pareto, was an early 20th century economist who postulated that a large share of wealth was owned by a small percentage of the population. He developed a mathematical formula that illustrated the unequal distribution of wealth in the country, observing that 20 percent of the people owned 80 percent of the wealth. As the idea progressed into improving quality it took on the notion that there are a 'vital few and a trivial many' areas of concern which eventually resulted in the 80/20 rule. As an example, there was a quality measurement that showed 20 percent of the defects in software were causing 80 percent of the problems experienced by users, or a sales team measurement showed that 80 percent of sales came from 20 percent of the sales force. The part of this formula that is important for a leader is to seek out the vital 20 percent that really matters and has the most impact when looking at a large set of information or trying to solve a problem.

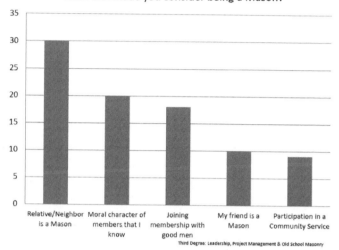

Figure 6: Pareto Chart

A Pareto Chart is represented by a series of bars whose heights reflect the frequency or impact of what is being measured. The bars (events) are arranged in descending order of height from left to right. This means the events represented by the tall bars on the left are relatively more frequent than those on the right. The Pareto Chart is used to visually separate the 'vital few' from the 'trivial.' Pareto Charts are useful because they can be used to show what factors have the greatest cumulative effect. Ideally, this allows the user to focus attention on the frequently occurring factors or events.

Constructing a Pareto Chart:

1. Start by brainstorming categories of information that impact the activity under review. Don't be concerned if you don't get them all, as you can expand the list during future iterations.

2. Collect raw data – Observe the activity and collect meaningful data that you observe which you believe impacts the activity. Focus on the categories brainstormed above, but you may find a trend if you capture other events. You can expect that your brainstorming, when performed by subject matter experts, will generate the most promising and critical categories. But through observation, you may find other areas to be reviewed.

3. Arrange the categories in descending order per the total number of occurrences. Construct and label bars for each category. Place the tallest bar at the far left, then the next tallest to its right and so on.

Analysis of the Pareto Chart - examine the first several bars. Look at the cumulative sum of the percentages for these bars. These will approach 80 percent, when the number of categories approaches 20 percent. Don't be too concerned if the 80/20 rule does not happen to be exactly correct in any individual case, sometimes there are factors that can skew the results. The importance of the effort is to highlight the critical categories.

After resolving the first couple of bars, recalculate the Pareto Chart through additional observation, as the solutions to the original issues, may have changed the overall distribution of what my remain. This process of solving a few bars and repeating the analysis can drive the right kind of improvement decisions.

Benchmarking

Another quality tool is benchmarking which uses comparisons to measure an organization's position or capability relative to other organizations performing the same or similar functions. When you identify a standard way for measuring a function, capability, service or industry for comparison, it is possible to gain perspective on an organization's relative performance. For example, there are standards for counting errors in software and for work practices in pharmacies, and also in hospitals, so it is possible in these businesses to compare one software company to another, one pharmacy to another, and one hospital to another. As there are standard ways of counting, these entities represent good candidates for benchmarking; there are lots of professions, industries and activities that have standards that make them good candidates for benchmarking.

To understand what makes the best, the best, consider using benchmarking. Benchmarking is especially valuable when there is relevant and good data available for comparison with a best-in-class organization. Including a person, a team, a company, a lodge or an organization that is the best, can provide greater insight into how you can emulate the best and can be the catalyst for you to innovate and become the best. Determine who is the very best at what you wish to be good at performing. Perform research to learn about the way similar businesses handle their particular expertise. Don't be afraid to ask them directly for the information. Many organizations that perform at a high level are continuously learning organizations and are willing to trade, barter or share information. If you can't get the information, consider contacting trade associations and research trade literature.

In the course of your benchmark research, look to determine which consistent standards are used to measure performance relevant to the process or activity you are looking to measure. If you don't know and can't determine the standard measured, benchmarking won't be a valuable experience. However, if you can find a common measure that helps to answer a common question, such as when a customer asks "What is the mean time between failures (MTBF) on your widget?", then you have a grand opportunity to utilize benchmarking.

It is not enough to only know that your MTBF is 120 hours on your standard widget and 150 hours for your deluxe widget, as you want to know if that number is good or bad. For the individual numbers without context have little value. Therefore, you also want to know where your competitors and best-in-class organizations stand. If you are competing against a company for an order, and that company has a MTBF of 100 hours (more hours between failures is better), you are probably okay from the perspective of MTBF. However, if their MTBF is 1,000 hours who do you think will get the order, all other things being equal?

Once you decide what to benchmark, and how to measure it, the object is to figure out how the best got to be the best and determine what steps you can take to become one of the best or to become the best.

You don't need to focus on industries or teams just like yours, as there are a lot of processes that are common among industries. For example, call-center behavior, accounting practices, janitorial-service efforts, software-development process steps, and marketing activities are usually not industry specific. These practices are good candidates for benchmarking across industries.

Monitoring and Control

The purpose of project monitoring and control is to provide an understanding of a projects status and to communicate a project's progress. This better enable a response, when the project's performance deviates significantly from the plan, and so that appropriate corrective actions can be taken. Project monitoring is performed continuously throughout the life of a project seeking to observe deviations from the expected. Project control is that aspect of the project management process wherein corrective and preventative actions are taken.

A vital part of monitoring is collecting information, which is gathering metrics. There are three basic types of metric data: quantitative data - which is raw data, qualitative indicator data - which is derived and calculated data, and prognoses trend data - which is projected values and predictions, which allows you to project values and predict future values.

Quantitative metrics are the result of observable information or other raw data sources. For instance, collecting data on the number of brothers who attended a volunteer event or the number of hours utilized in planning an event. An example of a qualitative indicator would be the average number of volunteer hours per member of the lodge. Prognostic data would be considering the trend at another lodge, if we send text and email reminders to the brothers, we can increase volunteer hours.

Here are five basic categories that can be used to identify possible quantitative metrics:

1. Time 2. Cost 3. People 4. Size 5. Quality

If you are not collecting and using metrics today, start! For most organizations, starting the metric collection journey beginning to collect information immediately is more valuable than spending a large amount of effort attempting to select the perfect data metrics to collect. As you will find, collecting metrics demands a certain level of discipline and effort. An important task for an organization is to develop the discipline to regularly collect data. The next task is to make use of the information to keep the team motivated to continue collecting data. With discipline in place, you can better expand and reassess the proper set of metric data to be collected.

Shortly after starting the collection of metrics, consider creating a metrics dictionary as a next step in developing organization discipline, where you describe what metrics are collected and how they are collected, so that the process will be repeatable, even if team members change responsibilities. Metric data definitions should explain what exactly is to be measured, how the item will be assessed and the units of measurement that will be used (such as percentages, numbers, ratios or indexes). Some organizations also believe that a metric data definition should include which person(s) and/or roles in the organization will, collect use and own the metric, as this encourages greater accountability for the collection and use of the data.

Metrics are also effective when multiple people collect the same data and you can compare figures. Also do research to determine if a metric has already been defined as an industry benchmark or has been captured by a lodge or is a regulatory guideline for your business. The payoff for this research can be a valuable investment in the growth of your metrics collection process.

Problem Solving Process

Become a standout at problem solving and decision making. This is a progressive step toward becoming a better leader. The role of a good leader is to help solve problems. Problem resolution can be accomplished systematically.

The process has six steps:

1.) Define the problem.
2.) Get the facts.
3.) Develop a list of options.
4.) Analyze the options.
5.) Select an option.
6.) Communicate selection and execute.

Problem Solving Process

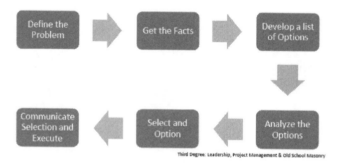

Third Degree: Leadership, Project Management & Old School Masonry

Figure 7: Problem Solving Process

Defining the problem is critically important. Words mean things, and in this context words limit and define the scope of the problem. Therefore, having the right problem statement bounds the remaining steps in the problem solving process and ultimately provides the test for the success of the solution. When defining a problem, attempt to define it so that it is balanced and therefore not too broad nor too narrow. After the problem statement is clear, spend some time to verify the completeness with the stakeholders.

Begin fact-finding. Finding the facts can be difficult and elusive and many times the evidence is not available because they were never captured or anticipated. If you ever have an opportunity to put a process in place to capture facts, data, statistics and other information relevant to making decisions in your business, it is a wise investment of your time and energy. Start with the end result in mind and consider what data is required to generate the type of decision or solution you need. Gathering the best information you can is important to getting to the right solutions, so don't skimp on getting the best information available.

To generate potential solutions when working alone or in a group, use formal brainstorming techniques. Also talk to team members, leaders, brothers, subject-matter experts and stakeholders to generate a list. On other occasions, collect research and solutions used by others in similar situations. The list of generated options can't be too long, however it can take too long to generate. Generating the list is important to be sure the breadth and scope of considerations is sufficiently broad. Out of the box thinking should be encouraged. Don't throw out an idea or a proposal too early. Sometimes you can build or feed off an idea to craft a more perfect solution.

Analyze your list of options. Consider the pros and cons of each option. Reduce the list as you go, removing the options that have the least probability for success. Get down to a small set of alternatives to give it a deeper consideration to further narrow the options.

Make a selection from your list and then support it with conviction. Many times, several options will work, but success will depend upon the conviction and effort put forth by those engaged in the implementation and execution of the solution. A big rule of caution at this step is to prevent a paralysis of analysis condition. Be sure to limit the time for the selection process and have an escape clause that forces a decision, for when the group can't or just won't make a decision.

Finally, tell the decision story. Tell how the team made the decision. Be sure every stakeholder and member of the implementation team has access to the information and then enable the team to go execute.

Internalize these process steps. Walk through the step in your head when addressing issues and concerns. Be deliberate, and leave no stone unturned in the execution of each step in the process. Ask questions to support a deep understanding for each of the steps in this process when attending meetings and addressing concerns. Share, in your conversations the thought process and analysis you have done. When time permits and you are leading or facilitating a group involved in problem solving formally walk them through the process.

Risk Management

Risk Management is an approach to determine what level of risk you are willing to accept relative to how much you are willing to invest to reduce your level of risk. You often can't reduce your risk level to zero. An example, of the risk management quandary that needs resolution: As

Worshipful Master you are responsible for the protection of lodge valuables so you generally lock the doors of the building when you exit. This is a method to reduce the risk that the lodge will be robbed and loss something of value. Yet the risk does not go to zero when you lock the door because there are other options for a thief who wants to get to your valuables. For example, they may use the windows, force the door, or utilize another entry point. If you want to reduce the risk more, you can consider an alarm system, but, with the additional risk reduction there is a cost, in this case both an initial cost and a continuous cost. So, additional tradeoffs will need to be considered. You will need to weigh the probability of a break-in against the cost of an alarm system. How much is it worth to reduce the risk? Of course, if you decide to purchase an alarm system, you again need to make decisions about the size and capabilities for the system. Do you only place sensors on the doors or do you also place sensors on the windows? What about upper floor or basement windows? Do you include motion detectors? Do you place key pads only at the one frequently used entrance, or all entrances? Do you place a key pad in the all rooms, the lodge room or a limited set of the most-frequently-used rooms? How large a battery (How many hours of charge will it hold)? What type(s) of horns and alarms?

A generic tool for managing the risk is to take an assessment of the risk itself. Then take an assessment of risk mitigation options.

Risk Management Template

Probability X Impact = Total

Risk Name	Probability	Impact	Total	Mitigation

Third Degree: Leadership, Project Management & Old School Masonry

Figure 8: Risk Management

Start by generate a list of risks. A gathering of subject-matter experts in a brainstorming session can deliver a respectable list of risks. For each item on the list, weigh the probability the risk will occur and then weigh the impact if the risk occurs. Using a scale of 1 to 9 for the occurrence probability and 1 to 9 for the impact is a way to weigh the level of risk between items on the risk list. Multiplying the two categories (probability and impact) will yield a weighted priority list.

You can also limit the weighting factors to something like high, medium and low, and respectively assign the values of 9, 3, and 1. This smaller set of options can reduce the amount of time expended on getting the weights perfect. To generate bigger spreads in the weights, you can use more values and larger spreads.

Starting at the higher-weighted risk items, develop ways to prevent the risk and estimate costs for implementing the prevention. With this information, you can decide if you want to invest in preventing the risk from becoming a problem.

As a leader, you need to look beyond the dollars and cents and not forget some of the intangibles, like loss of customer satisfaction, an inopportune time for the failure or the impact to the organization or your personal reputation.

When considering the probability of investing in risk prevention, also consider the cost of fixing a problem after it occurs. Sometimes it's just better to fix problems when they occur. This is seldom the case, but is special instances it is true. But, as a common adage in the risk management domain suggests, "If you don't have time to do it right, then when do you think you will have time to do it over again?" This is just a reminder that investing in producing quality is a good practice and on many occasions is cheaper than releasing something with a known or potential problem and then paying to fix the problem later.

Chapter Three – Master Mason

.

Chapter Four ~ Conclusion / Wrap-up

"Brother James, thanks for stopping by my home" said Samuel.

"Well Brother Gordon, thanks for accepting my request to talk. The Worshipful Master has called on us again" James stated, "He has asked us to participate in a Masonic college, in a couple of months. He still gets positive feedback on the article even though it has been several months since it was published. I suggested to the Worshipful Master that I would like for it to be a joint session with both you and I speaking and he agreed that might be a nice touch. So, I am here to ask for your assistance and participation. Can you help?"

Samuel leaned back and said, "It depends. When is the Masonic college?"

"It is scheduled for the second Saturday in a month-and-a-half and will be held at our Lodge. That will give us about seven weeks to prepare. The classes usually run for about three hours from 9:00 am to noon." James continued, "I don't think we need to prepare a lot as we can use the notes from the article to define the primary points of the presentation, which will be about leadership and Masonry. Our portion of the college is scheduled to be 90 minutes. In the article we talked about 15 Leadership Attributes; I have the list here."

James slid a list with the 15 items across the desk. It read:

1.) Be on time.
2.) Work hard.
3.) Be prepared.
4.) Know the goal.
5.) Love what you do.
6.) Study and know the fundamentals.
7.) Be friendly.
8.) Be collaborative.
9.) Be faithful.
10.) Be a constructive member of the team.
11.) Personal discipline.
12.) Be attentive.
13.) Take initiative.
14.) Be self-assured.
15.) Be your best.

"I'm thinking we can break the set into three slides, and arrange them in the order they were presented in the article." said James.

Samuel agreed and said, "That is great." He added, "I have been working on another presentation for a community board that I sit on and that presentation could perform double duty and add content to our Masonic College presentation. The community board presentation includes information on both leadership and project management."

"Here is a list of leadership topics that are covered."

1.) Strategic Planning
2.) Hiring Good People
3.) Servant hood
4.) Mentors
5.) Communications
6.) Confidence and Enthusiasm
7.) Balanced Communications
8.) Ethics and Etiquette

9.) Execution
10.) Integration
11.) Innovation and Managing Change
12.) Emotional Intelligence

After James had a chance to look over the leadership list, Samuel continued, "In addition, here are some project management tools that were given to me by a member of the project management office in my company who also happens to be a mentee,"

1.) Vision / Dream
2.) Wisdom
3.) The 5 W's
4.) SWOT Analysis
5.) QCD – Quality, Cost & Delivery
6.) Time Management
7.) SIPOC
8.) Stakeholder Analysis
9.) Quality
10.) Monitoring and Control
11.) Decision Making
12.) Risk Management

Samuel said, "I can pull together the slides and send them to you, by the end of the week."

"That's great, Samuel," James responded. "I would also like to add one more subject area, at the request of the Worshipful Master. While talking with the Junior Warden and Worshipful Master recently, they shared with me that we need to invest more energy in closing our projects more efficiently. They stated that while working with the Senior Warden on a couple of community-service projects and fundraisers, they noticed that we reinvent the wheel every time we host an event, even if it is the same program as the previous year. They shared that we don't collect and document information regarding what went well and what went wrong. We don't have good records on who participated, who paid, what vendors we used, actual costs and the like. And, we definitely don't have sufficient information to discuss trends over multiple years. Our lack of data and documentation is even more apparent when the chairperson changes from year to year. So, I'd like to add a slide or two on closing out a project. I can work with the Junior Warden this week and get something to you by Friday."

James continues, "This set of information will tell the story of leadership and Masonry, and will easily fill up the 90 minutes we have been allotted. I'm looking forward to sharing the information with our Brothers at the Masonic College."

Closing

When closing a project there are a couple of objectives, documenting the best and worst parts of the endeavor and officially ending the project.

Too often leaders fail to take the time to properly close a project, frequently because they are focused on the next project, solution or organizational activity. However, well-disciplined leaders and organizations have a record of their activities, learn from their past and share that learning within their ranks. The discipline of properly closing a project promotes the creation of a positive set of institutional knowledge. Remember the adage; the job is not finished until the paperwork is done.

A key to the successful use of closing documentation is creating a repository for storing the documentation and information from previous projects. The repository is then referenced when starting new projects and when estimating activities to enable more informed decisions. Do what you can to create and properly store the meaningful data from the project. Capture reports, minutes from meetings, financial information, presentations, and other information collected during your projects. This is the set of data that can help a leader to take advantage of the organizations successes and to avoid repeating its mistakes.

To formally close a project and prevent creeping elegance or a never-ending set of additions and new requirements, be sure the project has an end. The tried and true method for closing large projects is hosting a celebration to acknowledge the completion of a project. Celebrate with a party, a trip, or the formal recognition of the members of the team. For the normal closing of a project, there is a final meeting or a closing report that will be rendered or distributed. All can serve as a closing marker.

The Closing Degree

For a Mason, there is no project, and there is no closure, until his transition from the terrestrial to the celestial. For a well lived Masonic life is a continuous and ever-evolving process of self reflection and self improvement. There are several areas of a Masonic life that should be diligently observed, reviewed and enhanced. The foundation is a deep knowledge and understanding of the ritual, which is supported by interpreting the symbolism of the fraternity. A Masonic life includes how an individual engages his obligation of charity and the overall philosophy of the fraternity, which is a daily test of his Masonic conduct. Jurisprudence and etiquette provide rigor and consistency for the Masonic body.

Finally, knowing your lodge history and the origins of the fraternity is a necessary component of telling the full story of Masonry.

All of the leadership, project management and Masonry, is about living for the magic moments in life. A lot of what we are and what we do is about living for the special moments and occasions in life. To get to the magic and special times, you wade through the ordinary times. But, then, it happens, on an ordinary trip to the nursing home to visit an elderly Brother, whom you barely know. You've stopped by his home a couple of times to drop off tickets or other things, but never really talked. He is older, a generation or more ahead of you in age. The nurse comes in to bring dinner. He is having a little trouble feeding himself because his hand shakes, so you offer to help. At the end you place a spoonful of applesauce, up to his lips. You look up to see tears in his eyes and you have the moment, both of you. In that moment, you recognize why you have participated, and endured and gladly given your time to Masonry. It was for that moment of brotherly connection, and you are hooked on Masonry, for life.

In business there are moments that highlight the fruits of leadership and project management, that you will remember all of your life. You will remember that moment when the project you sponsored has its first product rolling off the assembly line, or that moment when you learned that helping your team to solve a problem led them to the President's club for the quality of their work or your mentee earned a handshake from the president of the company due to your influence and the quality of their work. These enduring moments are why we lead, why we plan, and why we are invested in improving our leadership skills.

These are the moments that give your efforts toward personal improvement value. That makes all of life's ups and downs worth enduring. These moments are what make leadership and leading a team to a goal, an incredible experience.

My friends if you are not already associated with the fraternity of Freemasons, ladies consider joining the Order of Eastern Stars and Gentlemen

2B1 ASK1

Amen - So Mote It Be

Chapter Four – Closing / Wrap-up

The best project
you will ever
work on is you!

About the Author

John R. Hill, Jr., is a member of Eureka Lodge #36, Free and Accepted Masons, Prince Hall, in the great state of New York and has been a member for more than 29 years. He has served his lodge by holding many elected and appointed offices including twice as Worshipful Master. He has served in a variety of appointed offices at the state level, and been elected as a trustee for the corporation that manages a property that houses a youth camp, supported by the Masons and Order of Eastern Star. John is a founding member of the Frederick Douglas Toastmasters Club #6898.

John received a Computer Engineering degree from Boston University, and has worked as an individual contributor, designing hardware and writing software, and as a manager during his 30-year career. John is an inventor on four patents. He has received his Project Management Professional Certification in 2002 and his ITIL® Foundations Certification in 2012.

John has served in a leadership role for numerous community organizations in Rochester, NY. He has served as Board President for Big Brothers and Big Sisters of Greater Rochester, NY, and as Chair of a leadership development program within the United Way of Greater Rochester.

Made in the USA
Middletown, DE
31 January 2015